Portraits
of
Japan

ADRIAN WALLER

His *Japan Times Weekly* writings

Volume 2

YOHAN PUBLICATIONS, INC.

PORTRAITS OF JAPAN

A YOHAN LOTUS BOOK/Published 1992

Copyright © 1992 by Adrian Waller

YOHAN PUBLICATIONS, INC.

14-9 3-chome, Shinjuku-ku, Tokyo, Japan

Printed in Japan

Books by Adrian Waller

Theatre on a Shoestring

Adrian Waller's Guide to Music

Data for a Candlelit Dinner

The Gamblers

Soulikias: Portrait of an Artist

*Writing! An informal, anecdotal guide to the secrets of
   crafting and selling non-fiction*

The Canadian Writer's Market,
   Eighth Revised Edition

No Ordinary Hotel
   The Ritz-Carlton's first seventy-five years

Who Stole The Rainbow?

The Canadian Writer's Market,
   Ninth Revised Edition

Being Here, a Western journalist's view of Japan
   (A collection of Japan Times Weekly *columns)*

Portraits of Japan
   (Japan Times Weekly *writings, Volume 2*)

*For my wife Irene, whose
inspiration was
a guiding light.*

CONTENTS

Acknowledgements

I am indebted to Keisuke Okada, editor of *The Japan Times Weekly*, and Mike Millard, the general editor, both of whom fought so hard to keep my column alive when certain powers that be objected to the way it criticized Japan and its institutions, and to my wife, Irene, and my daughter, Nathalie, who constantly helped me find and refine my topics.

My thanks also go to the remainder of the hard-working *Weekly* staffers who encouraged me while reaching for new personal heights against odds that often seemed insurmountable and to David Bernat, who proofread my work and made valuable suggestions in the process.

Finally, how could I possibly forget my readers, without whom my work at *The Weekly* would have been superfluous?

Introduction

NO ONE WAS MORE surprised than I was when the first volume of my *Japan Times Weekly* columns, published by Yohan as *Being Here, a Western journalist's view of Japan,* was so well received. I first began writing my column in the warm spring of 1991, barely six months after I had arrived in Tokyo from Montreal, where I then lived and worked — mainly as a magazine writer, author, and university teacher — merely as small pieces that were part of a general renovation plan to help give *The Weekly* a new and broader personality. Quite honestly, I did not intend them to be anything more than that.

In that first book, however, my little columns, and some of the larger pieces that were also included, reached across the Pacific, primarily to bookstores in Los Angeles and San Francisco, and were met there with some enthusiasm — as they were throughout Japan. So a second volum *Portraits of Japan,* seemed logical.

As I have explained several times during the past three years, the actual idea for the column, originally called "Being Here," and what it should try to do, came about in a Tokyo coffee shop one afternoon when my colleague editor Mike Millard and I were devising a course we felt *The Weekly* might follow if it were to be better than it already was. I like to think that what I began to write then, and maintained week in and week out, made a lot of readers happy.

If my frankness in portraying Japan as I saw it made some of them unhappy or uncomfortable, however, that is fine, too. Western journalism is predicated on the very simple assumption that all is not right in the world, and that it is the job of a columnist to bring the wrongs into full public view, either through humor or through the "straight" reporting of important issues.

I have always sought to do both to the best of my ability, but it was not possible, it should be pointed out, without some uncharacteristic Japanese confrontation from time to time. A handful of *Japan Times* editors objected to my criticisms of their country and its institutions, even those whose ability to recognize the color and innuendo of the English language was questionable.

I learned to cope, though. One thing imperative for living, let alone for making a mark in the workforce, is to be able to convert negatives into positives; so whenever certain editors complained about one of my columns, I sensed that it must have been a good one!

Many Japanese readers, however — and, of course, a discerning Japanese publisher — felt that my comments were perfectly valid, and it was people such as these who kept my spirits intact.

I am not about to continue this debate here, except to add that press censorship in Japan is very subtle and very real. It is something experienced Western journalists who take pride in their profession constantly worry about. I can honestly say, though, that with the help of Keisuke Okada, my understanding Japanese editor at *The Japan Times Weekly*, and, of course, my colleague Mike Millard, I was able to cast censorship aside.

Everything I wanted to say was printed — that is, until I resigned my editorship on June 17, 1992, my 56th birthday.

Fortunately, however, I had produced enough work for another book. Thus, you are holding *Portraits of Japan*, and I hope you will enjoy reading it as much as I have enjoyed putting it all together for you.

Adrian Waller,
Tokyo, 1992

Foreword

WHEN ADRIAN WALLER disappeared from the North American writing scene in the fall of 1989, he was conspicuous by his sudden absence. He was one of the rare people who had been able to elevate magazine writing to an art form, and his books on just how to do this are legendary. Soon, there was news that he had gone to work for a Japanese English-language newspaper, which, for many of us, was a surprise, inded!

The reasons eventually became obvious to us. In addition to his day-to-day editing work, Waller was shrewdly churning out a column that was worthy of a book or two, and, in its own little way, was fast becoming as controversial as the uneven playing field that has come to describe the problems of Japan-U.S. trade relations.

Adrian Waller's column was controversial in Japan, I should add, because apart from being exquisitely written, it was also so refreshingly honest. And honesty, as I recall from the time I represented a consortium of British newspapers and American business magazines in Tokyo throughout the 1970s and much of the early 1980s, is not what Japanese journalism is all about.

That said, it is ironic that Waller's fate should subsequently lay in the hands of a group of Japanese journalists who wielded some influence at *The Japan Times*, not because they had any special ability, but because they had been in the paper's employ for some time and were, therefore, automatically afforded a loud voice, and one that opposed Waller's views.

Yet it was these, laid out, as they always were, in a lively and attractive writing style almost everyone could understand, that won Waller his big cluster of fans within *The Japan Times Weekly's* modest circulation. To many of these readers, Waller *was The Weekly*, and when he left in June 1992, a large part of this perfectly respectable publication (much better now than it was when I first saw it all those years ago) doubtless departed with him.

If there is another irony here, it is this: Waller felt that Japan would never fully internationalize until its journalism improved — until Japan had become sufficiently democratic as to allow journalism to speak to and from the heart rather than to and from the corporate ideology. Waller also felt that there was far too much business writing in Japan; not enough words were being spent on the deepening human predicament there.

In this view, he was by no means alone. While his opponents were busily damning him— even trying to dissuade him from writing, if you can believe that — academics were equally committed to praising his work as being exceptional. Most notable of these was Dr. Howard Roiter, author of the best-selling book *Voices From The Holocaust*, and a professor of English at the University of Montreal. Roiter said of Waller's columns: "They are absolutely brilliant — wonderfully crafted pieces!" In Japan, meanwhile, teachers at various colleges and universities subscribed to *The Weekly* not just because it had become an interesting, spunky publication with a personality of its own, but so that their students could read Waller to practice their English and sharpen their minds.

Adrian Waller's columns are far from being merely linguistically masterful. They contain a great deal of humor and deep insights into how the Japanese think and act. They are unusually perceptive pieces, and almost all the ideas behind them were inspired by the author's every-day travels to and from his office, and doubtless to other parts of the country. For me, it is remarkable that many of his columns, and one or two of his larger pieces, were literally written overnight!

If there is one overriding theme in the collection presented here, it is that all is not well in Japan. As I recall from my own dealings there, it is a place that mixes the pain it invokes through racism, not to mention the most awful corruption, with the intrinsic pleasures of a gentle, age-old culture and the deep-felt kindness expressed by most of its people nearly all of the time. By fusing these elements in a way that could be understood across oceans, Adrian Waller has been proven absolutely right in his assessment of what a cross-cultural column should do. He is the first to admit, however, that his senior colleague, an American, encouraged him to use his column to bridge Japan with the West, and, even though this was to little avail in the eyes of the Japanese management at the newspaper, Waller will always be grateful for this help.

In summary, Adrian Waller's *Japan Times Weekly* writings truly are world-class, and it was a sad day for a lot of people when his column was snatched from him without so much as a chance to bid his readers a fond farewell. The good news is that the best of these pieces are reproduced here for all of us to read, re-read, and cherish.

__Jon Malcolm Tierney__
New York City, 1992

A Comedy of Terrors

February 1, 1992

IT WAS A SIGHT to behold — the dynamic, yet quietly persuasive Japanese actress Komaki Kurihara telling some of the world's most powerful politicians that they were also among the most corrupt. And in case you didn't see it on television early on Wednesday evening, for it was removed from later newscasts in what may have been an act of self-censorship, it happened at the Liberal-Democratic Party's regular convention that afternoon. During her 10-minute speech, Kurihara pleaded, "Please show us the truth, not artifice. Conspiracy and betrayal should be left to Shakespeare."

As television cameras panned the auditorium, and a sea of blue suits and silver ties, many of the men there looked sheepish, to say the least. Some, even the grayest among them, found the strength and the audacity to heckle Kurihara as if she were speaking untruths that were completely out of line. Let them heckle and catcall, I say. And you probably do, too.

Kurihara's speech, of course, came only a couple of hours after the Tokyo District Court agreed to a request, by the Tokyo District Public Prosecutor's Office, to extend the detention of Fumio Abe, a member of the House of Representatives, no less, and both a friend of Prime Minister Kiichi Miyazawa and the former secretary general of his LDP faction.

As you read this, the slick, bespectacled Abe may

either be packing his suitcase to go home, or might even be there already — recovering from the ordeal of his interrogation. It's worth recalling here that he was arrested on Jan. 13 for allegedly receiving bribes of some ¥80 million from the bankrupt steel frame maker, Kyowa Corp, while he was director of the Hokkaido and Okinawa Development Agency. The police have needed a lot of time to find out whether or not — when he denied receiving those bribes — he was lying.

At any rate, when the ordinary session of the Diet resumed on Friday, Abe was conspicuous by his absence because the court had granted the prosecutor's request to hold him in the Tokyo Detention Center for an extra 10 days. Thus Abe became the second Diet member to be detained from the session because of a criminal investigation in 25 years. The last such case involved the late Katsutoshi Sekiya. When the Diet resumed that year, he was in custody in connection with the 1967 taxi corruption case in Osaka.

Miyazawa, a master of understatement, told delegates at that same LDP convention at which actress Kurihara spoke so eloquently, and without a prepared text, that Abe's arrest was "quite regrettable," and that it should be "taken seriously." He then expressed an unyielding determination to carry out some sort of political reform, and added that a code of political ethics needed to be established urgently — as well as "a system" in which "money is not so pivotal, and in which elections focus on policy."

Really? I think all of Japan — and half the globe — is wondering why something like this wasn't put into place some years ago. But then, as Karel van Wolferen says in the opening passages of his book, *The Enigma of Japanese Power*, "Japan perplexes the world. It has become a major power, yet it does not behave the way most of the world expects a world power to behave; sometimes it gives the impression of not wanting to belong to the world at all."

The problem, of course, is that Japan has such a long tradition of repaying one favor with another, and bandying gifts about, that it is becoming increasingly harder to determine what, in fact, is a present from the bottom of a soft, well-meaning heart, and what is a bribe. So Miyazawa may soon have to dream up some kind of legislation that will make Japanese tradition and customs more applicable to modern times.

Anyway, the system he envisioned, he said, was "the only way to win back the confidence of rank and file party members and other party supporters." Of course, he mentioned nothing about instilling confidence in the public at large, and that, we can suppose, is why Komaki Kurihara took it upon herself to say what she did.

She was on pretty safe ground. The stream of LDP politicians involved in irregular dealings seems endless. This week, opposition parties were arming themselves to question Miyazawa not only about Abe, but about his own involvement in the Recruit shares-for-favors scandal. They were also planning to ask him about a more recent matter, the full extent of which has yet to be disclosed. What is known so far is that more than 100 politicians — most of them LDP members — are suspected of having received huge political contributions from the major freight service group, Tokyo Sagawa Kyubin.

So when actress Komaki Kurihara likens Diet goings-on to a Shakespearean drama, she's not far wrong. But which play, exactly? *Much A Do About Nothing*? Hardly. *A Comedy of Errors*? Maybe. More certain is that in all of Shakespeare's plays, good triumphs over evil, honesty over corruption. But this sordid drama — being acted out in the Diet, no less — has yet to have an ending.

Women: Abused by culture

May 9, 1992

THERE IS AN IRONY HERE, and it's not hard to fathom:
The richer Asia has become, the more its women have
suffered. If they do not fall victim to the burgeoning sex
industry, they have a terrible time being accepted as
complete, capable, and deserving people.

To be recognized, Japanese women must work
twice as hard as men, and, during this time, must
content themselves with all manner of menial jobs,
like making tea, photocopying, and generally being
pretty corporate hostesses. Some Japanese companies
will not hire divorced women with children, perceiving
them as being unsteady and disloyal. Nor do they often
want single women who live away from their families,
considering them too independent and frivolous to
be of any use.

Japanese women get paid less than Japanese men,
even though they may do the same job better, and
almost never get responsible jobs because it is also
widely thought that they will one day leave to marry.
An orphaned Japanese woman has almost no chance of
marriage because she no longer belongs to an intact
family, a culturally important element in the matrimonial contract. Those women who want to continue
working after marriage — if they are lucky enough to
find jobs that are compatible with their intellectual
capabilities — all too often suffer the indignity of

having to get their husband's permission. Some companies, meanwhile, have been known to term women who are older than 25 as "Christmas cake," and see absolutely nothing wrong with firing them and replacing them with younger women who may be less brainy, but more ornamental.

Against all of this, the amount of sexual harassment against women of all ages in Japan is staggering, and it is usually unreported because most victims still believe that it is their duty to succumb to a man's advances. Far too many do not want to talk about this, fearing for their jobs.

Why do Japanese men treat women this way? Beyond the obvious reason — that because women here have learned to be submissive men know they can get away with it — there is a broader cultural context that has to be considered. Under certain laws instigated by long-ago emperors, women were exported to other Asian countries — as prostitutes. In 1528, a public prostitution system was established in Japan because it was considered unethical for a married couple to enjoy sexual pleasure together. Thus began a sort of prostitution culture and, coupled with deep-rooted sexist and patriarchal attitudes influenced by Confucianism (these said that women were always to obey a father, a husband, and her eldest son), men learned to regard women as lesser beings.

From this grew a disquieting male logic that infiltrates every segment of daily living today. Men think that women are fair game for sexual abuse and discrimination because of their "prostitute-like nature," whatever this means. Conversely, it accounts for the way many women still believe that to succumb to a man's sexual advances is something that is expected of them.

Given this scenario, it is not hard to see other, more blatant examples of female maltreatment — those that inspired the formation, in March 1977, of a group called the Asian Women's Association. Japan had not only raped its neighbors militarily, the association felt, but was now sending planeloads of men to neighboring countries to do it sexually.

Why Japanese men and not those from, say, Australia or America? Well, some have been Australians and Americans. Most, though, have been Japanese who — with submissive, uncomplaining wives at home — suddenly found they had a lot of money to spend, and that there were a lot of attractive, impoverished women in such places as Korea, Thailand, and the Philippines.

In another popular sex-tour destination, Taiwan, a travel agent named Nathaniel S. Lin, who works for Seika Travel Service, decided to try to do something about it. When he discovered that Tokyo travel agents were organizing men-only sex-tour packages that included flight, hotel room, meals, sightseeing, and the services of young prostitutes who met clients at airports, he was so incensed that he personally financed an advertisement in a Japanese travel industry trade paper:

Dear Travel Agents of Japan. Do you know the word "shame"? Please do not ignore the fact that part of your salary, business, and dividend originates from money squeezed out of women who sell their bodies to Japanese tourists.

After several months, however, the trade paper refused to carry the advertisement, bowing to pressure from its subscribers. Most of these, of course, were the very people who are selling sex tours, which, today, constitute a bigger business than ever.

And consider this: Throughout nearly all of Asia, Japanese companies use women as a cheap — very cheap — source of labor, mostly on assembly lines. Then, for their vacations, their employees "buy" another segment of the female populations as prostitutes. Not only that, Japanese agents, working with Thais or Filipinos, seek out the women, while Japanese travel agents, mostly in Tokyo, organize the packages in conjunction with Japanese airlines and Japanese hotels.

According to government studies, of the 3 million Japanese men who travel abroad — and alone — as soon as they get one of their semi-annual company bonuses, about 97 percent go to Bangkok, and 85 percent to Manila. Despite the very serious threat of AIDS, says a recent Reuters news agency report, as many as 80 percent of these men have sex with a prostitute.

Don't rely too much on governments to do anything about it, though, because the financial stakes are too high. The Thai government, for example, has done nothing to stop a growing number of girls, some as young as 12, from dropping out of school to satisfy the needs of foreign men. In South Korea, the government allowed young women to flock to Cheju Island when, it was announced, it would become a tourist gambling resort that would cater almost exclusively to the kind of Japanese men Professor Renato Constantino of the

University of the Philippines calls "Imperial soldiers in civilian clothes."

Wealthy nations have always behaved badly, of course. That's how many of them became wealthy in the first place. Now, though, we are living in an age of enlightenment, and it is this enlightenment that can be our salvation. It seems to me that Japan, which has tried so hard in recent times to become a respectable member of the world community, should become a leader in stopping some of this abuse against women in neighboring Asian countries. And it should start at home — by casting off those antiquated traditions that relegate women to sex machines.

Despite laws that seek to control it, prostitution is widely considered a socially necessary evil. If it is true that prostitution really is a "socially necessary" evil, why is it that throughout most of Asia, only the women are punished, and rarely the men who rent their bodies? It is shameful beyond words, of course, and may not change until younger, more benevolent people — men and women together — take the reigns of Japan firmly in their hands and steer it from the Third World mentality that, in this respect, has made it the way it is.

Eventually, when women in Japan are finally considered man's equal, the workplace will become a much more equitable place, and male-only sex tours will not only become unfashionable, but be viewed with disdain as being slavish and downright demeaning. I hope it will happen soon.

Help — as a group

February 8, 1992

THE OTHER NIGHT, while on my way to return a movie to the local video rental store, I came upon a motorist in trouble on an ice-bound hill. As hard as he tried to escape — pumping the accelerator of his station wagon, and manipulating the steering wheel, both with agitation — he couldn't. And he was in immediate danger of sliding backwards and striking the car parked behind.

Troubled motorists of winter are by no means unfamiliar to me. I have spent about half my life in Canada, after all, where many drivers carry all manner of paraphernalia in the trunks, or boots, of their vehicles that can be used to free them should they be trapped, either in a snow bank or on a slippery surface — salt with which to melt thin ice, chains to wrap around tires, or grate-like contraptions that can be placed under a wheel that is spinning uselessly — all to provide traction.

Indeed, most Canadians learn — often the hard way — how to cope with winter driving, and when I saw the man in trouble, some of that learning came into play instantly.

You do not need special language skills, after all, to ask a motorist if he needs a push and that if I were to help in this way, he, as the driver, would need to put the station wagon into second gear, not first, so that the wheels would spin more slowly. It is not too difficult to demonstrate how it is easier to "rock" a vehicle free when it is trapped on ice rather than try to drive it away at high speed.

Anyway, I pushed and shoved for quite 20 minutes before the station wagon was clear of the car behind it. But reaching the ice-clear center of the road seemed almost impossible. By this time, my strength was waning a little, my back was aching, and I had been showered from head to foot with ice that was turning to water. Then, suddenly, something quite remarkable happened — for Japan, that is. A group of passersby came to my aid!

From experience — heaving huge pieces of luggage up and down station steps and carrying newly bought appliances to my home in big boxes — I have encountered very few volunteer helpers. It seems that the Japanese, particularly the men among them, do not volunteer instantaneously lest they might be perceived as breaking ranks in their group society.

There have, of course, been exceptions. Once, my briefcase burst open on the Yamanote Line, scattering the contents everywhere, and a cluster of salarymen leaped from their seats and helped me retrieve papers, spare socks, cassettes, pens, and spare underwear in time for me to leave the train at the next stop. When a friend tripped and cut her head at Seibu-Shinjuku station one morning, however, no one — I repeat, no one — came to her aid. Why?

A much-traveled Japanese neighbor tells me that my theory of a volunteer feeling afraid of breaking away from society to help — particularly in such a public place as a railway station or a street — is absolutely correct. "A Japanese usually needs a lot of courage to do a thing like that," she says. But, she adds, when one person   stops to help someone in need, another will surely follow — as a group. Soon, a lot of people will be helping, and together they will be a busy, concerned army of kindly helpers completely unconcerned about having departed from their society at large.

This is what I believe, and this is exactly what happened the other night on that ice-bound hill. The extra help of four young men enabled the man to drive away his station wagon in only two minutes or so, and, at this point, I continued my walk to the video rental store feeling perfectly good about having assisted someone in trouble.

I like to think, jokingly, of course, that there was some commentary in the film I was returning —*All Champions Forever*, a documentary that recalled the heyday of such heavyweight boxers as Muhammad Ali, Kenny Norton, Joe Frazier, and George Foreman, and told how, on their best days in the ring, all were capable of beating each other, which they did.

On leaving the store, I was in for a surprise — and another of those cultural niceties with which I must learn to deal. The station wagon driver was waiting to see me. "Thank you, thank you," he said in a flurry of bows, and poked a carton of cigarettes at me. Recalling the times passersby had helped me as a motorist when I was in trouble, I did not want to take his gift.

"No. It's OK," I said repeatedly. "Really it is." But then I also remembered how refusing a gift from a Japanese can sometimes be offensive. So I accepted my reward graciously and walked home musing on yet another one of those strange paradoxes that make Japan what it is. Why is it culturally unacceptable for me to tip a good waitress, yet perfectly all right for me to receive a gift for helping someone out?

I felt then, as I do now, that one good turn deserves another. And I know that the folks who have helped me free my car from snow and ice over the years are far too numerous to count.

One pet hate

WHILE RELAXING in a Mr. Donut the other day, I was approached by a high school student in a white blouse and a dark blue tunic. There was panic in her voice. "Excuse me, sir," she said. "Will you help me?" I must look like a benevolent old professor these days because a lot of people want my help. Japanese people have even begun to ask me for directions.

At first, I thought the girl had lost her bus fare home and wanted me to give her some money, which I would have done, gladly. Instead, she thrust her English textbook at me, and added, "I don't understand this."

She was pointing at a sentence that I thought rather odd: *"Mary's pet hate is living in the city."*

The girl's question was "What does 'pet hate' mean?"

I thought the text odd because you can't really teach such phrases until you have explained "pet" and "hate" separately, as nouns — and how "hate" can sometimes be used as a verb and "pet" can, as it is in this case, be an adjective.

Anyway, why teach young students idioms so early when they should be concentrating on forming clear sentences? I have always believed that Japanese schools should teach standard English first — and, God knows, that can take forever — and let the students discover the figures of speech and the colloquialisms for themselves as they begin to speak regularly with English-speaking people.

Talking of this, when I first arrived in Japan, I thought I was unique until every other foreigner I met on the trains, in the parks, at festivals, and in the squat Tokyo coffee houses, shared similar experiences of Japanese people wanting to practice their English with them. Every day for several weeks, and always at six minutes after noon, the telephone at the foreigners' house in which I lived with my wife and daughter rang, and when I picked it up — as I usually did, because I wasn't then working during the day — a small voice said, "Hello. My name is Keiko. What is yours?"

One day, Keiko didn't call. And the following day, when the phone rang once more, at exactly the same time, a pleasant, young voice announced, in exactly the same tone, and with the same innocence of expression, "Hello. My name is Junko. What is yours?"

These were teenage girls, I surmised, on a lunch break from their classes in a school somewhere in Tokyo. I was very sorry when, one day, the Japanese landlord answered the phone himself and told them not to call again because they were disturbing his tenants. As far as I was concerned, they weren't a nuisance at all. For me, having just arrived in Tokyo, they were my bridge with a culture I had read and heard a lot about and longed to know better.

Not only that, I visualize the courage these girls must have mustered to pick up the telephone to speak to someone they did not know. And courage must never be suppressed. Neither, of course, must the will to practice English.

IT IS NOW AN international story with all the makings of a newer-than-ever version of *Beauty and the Beast* . At least, that's what newspapers in French-speaking Quebec, Canada, are saying about the engagement of sumo wrestler Konishiki to 26-year-old Sumika Shioda. And why shouldn't it be news across the world? It has intrigue, romance, a certain element that is much larger than life as we know it, and some very weighty facts.

At 236 kg, the gargantuan Konishiki, 27, is 186 kg heavier than Sumika. She's a wisp of a woman — a model, in fact — who weighs a mere 50 kg. "For a long time," she says, somewhat timidly, "I have tried to hide from public view because of the big difference in our sizes. But I can do it no more. The truth is out, and we love each other."

Meanwhile, Konishiki, a Hawaiian whose real name is Salevaa Atisanoe, says that his marriage to Sumika, which will take place later this month, will certainly not stunt his efforts to reach new levels in sumo. His sights are set on becoming a Yokozuna, sumo's highest rank. First, though, he hopes that his marriage will appeal to the good graces of Tokyo immigration officials. He is asking them to grant him Japanese nationality so, like a lot of us, he doesn't have to present himself for a new working visa every year.

Good luck to him, and to his fiancée.

- *Author's note: Konishiki and Sumika were married in February 1992.*

Teaching English in Tokyo

July 28, 1990

NOT LONG AGO, Chisa Hashimoto, a 40-year-old Tokyo concert pianist and instructor at the Toho Gakuen Music University, enrolled in a course at the Shinjuku branch of an English conversation school called ASA. "I really wanted to refine my grammar so I could write good letters," she says. But, after spending ¥390,000, she discovered that she rarely saw the same teacher twice. She also ascertained that she probably knew more about the English language — and how to teach — than virtually all those staffers to whom she was eventually introduced. So she quit.

"The whole experience," says Hashimoto, "raised questions in my mind about who should be allowed to teach English — or anything else — in Japan." One of her friends, meanwhile, a woman named Hiromi Saito, confided that she had spent a similar amount of money at Berlitz, and with equal disappointment.

In reality, of course, a woman like Hashimoto, who already spoke and wrote English better than most American high school students, probably should not have enrolled in ASA. Nor should her friend have sought out Berlitz — even though, in fairness, this school spends a lot of time measuring students' abilities and tailoring programs to their individual needs. Both women became victims of a system that leaves the students and those teachers who take their work seri-

ously both disappointed and bemused. Says Coral
Harris, whose Executive Education hires only instructors who have documented Western experience
so it can satisfy some of Tokyo's best corporate
clients, "The Japanese — the students and the
language schools alike — must decide whether they
want grammar or glamor."

Fifteen years ago, there were between 600 and 800
language and conversation schools in Tokyo alone.
Since then, as the rush to learn English has intensified, the number has soared dramatically — to as
many as 9,000. And that, Harris says, excludes the
literally hundreds of conversation bars that every
realtor and his uncle are opening virtually overnight."

Basically, these schools fall into two broad categories.
First, there are the colleges that teach writing, conversation, and reading. One of these is Tokyo Foreign
Language College, which sets its own entrance
examinations, and hires qualified teachers, preferably
those with training in teaching English as a second
language, known in the business as ESL. TFLC also
tutors its 2,000 students in what is going on in the world
at large, and how to prepare for specific professions.
Among the 87 schools in Tokyo that are officially
recognized by the Japanese government's Education
Ministry, it trains tour guides, for instance, interpreters,
and secretaries, and offers popular courses in hoteliery,
international travel, and word processing.

Second, there are the conversation schools that
provide a friendly environment in which students may
practice the English they learned in high school, from

teachers who have not necessarily learned to speak it. These teachers try to help their clients brush up their grammar and expand their vocabularies, and generally have a good time. Sometimes the schools tend to masquerade as "proper" schools, and they have also proliferated in Tokyo since the rush to learn English, and to teach it, intensified in the early 1980s.

Done properly, however, teaching is far from easy. In fact, for the teacher, experienced or otherwise, it can be frustrating, indeed, and often unedifying. "We've all taught group classes," says Linda Palter, of New York City, who has been teaching for 11 years, "in which half the people understand what you are saying, perfectly, and the other half don't. You are left wondering how to involve everyone in an intelligent, entertaining, and instructive way."

Thereby hangs the dilemma.

When, or if, it is solved, English language teaching in Japan will be the richer for it — for everyone. While one side of language teaching may well be honorable (good schools offering a rich curriculum), the other is all too frequently shady: questionable sales tactics — intense, high-pressure telephone blitzes, for example, with persistent follow-ups that are designed to recruit even the reticent.

Like most of its competitors, a conversation school called Bi-Lingual charges its students about ¥8,000 for each 40-minute session, depending on how many they buy. It also tells many prospective clients that they will speak English fluently after only 25 lessons. And they are not alone. Nova sales people have been known to make the same promises. Additionally, Bi-Lingual's

"Royal Club," offers English lessons 24 hours a day. It costs ¥50,000 to join, and a further ¥300,000 for three months of tuition, the company says. But a teacher shakes his head in disbelief. "No, that's wrong," he says. "Most people pay about two million yen."

These schools are making a lot of money out of "teaching" English to the Japanese — billions of yen annually. And to ensure that the cash pours in, they are earnestly aiming to satisfy their students' needs at the expense of good teaching.

These needs are as diverse as the teachers themselves. "In essence," says Catherine Tansey, president of the Tokyo chapter of the Japan Association of Language Teachers (JALT), "conversation schools exist for two reasons. On the one hand, a lot of Japanese want to build their linguistic confidence, and think that conversation schools are the right place for it; on the other, even more people attend them to satisfy a hobby." Adds TFLC professor Irene Ben, "Students want to be able to tell their friends that they're learning English and are associating with foreigners. They don't really care if they learn English or not."

She's right, of course.

Many are known to pile into English conversation classes hoping to meet foreign teachers who will marry them, bored housewives are often seeking foreign friends, and many of the corporate schools that advertise for women teachers who are under 29 are places where businessmen know they can encounter blondes. Meanwhile, other clients cluttering these institutions are part of a Japanese phenomenon — thousands of people who like to study purely for the sake of it. "There may not be a real need or use for what they are learning" says Tansey, "but they will continue on because education to them has a value in itself."

Conversely, conversation schools try to satisfy their serious students, too — businessmen who are earnestly trying to learn sufficient English for an important business trip to, say, Los Angeles or London, and ambitious university graduates wanting to master the language, written and spoken, so they may broaden the horizons of a brilliant international career. But unfortunately, as Linda Palter says, the serious and the nonchalant not only end up in the same school, but in the same group classes, thus rendering them virtually useless because of what Tansey calls "a conflict in goals."

It is hard, for example, for teachers to set class goals when one half of the students can express themselves reasonably well, and the other half can't. Indeed, goals are so integral to teaching that the ways of reaching them distinguish the professional tutor from the rank amateur.

Enter here another disconcerting element in English teaching in Japan. "A goal for too many teachers," says Tansey, "is merely to complete a text book. Once the students have been through the book, they are presumed, by the school, the teacher, and themselves, to have been properly taught." Nothing could be more wrong. Experienced educators know that each of the more than 10,000 books that has been published specifically for the English teaching market is merely a tool of their profession, to be used as an aid. Says Tansey, "We must teach the students enough about language learning so they may set their own goals and make these known to their teachers."

To be fair, some of the better language schools do establish student levels — low, intermediate, and high — but a lot don't, because they do not know how to. Thus, an increasing number of students — like Chisa Hashimoto and her friend — have discovered, as have experienced foreign teachers, that many instructors at schools like ASA, and indeed such others as Nova, Bi-Lingual, and Plady House, are not really in the profession of teaching. They can't be. They haven't enough staffers with enough training.

"You really mean these schools hire anyone?" asks Junko Sakamoto, who is paying nearly ¥7,000 per 40-minute session at Berlitz. When contacted by telephone, the company refused to comment on this. Again to be fair, however, it is worth mentioning that Berlitz is known for screening its staff and for training them — for eight days.

And the people at ASA say that they have recently recruited several dozen professional teachers from Britain. "We really do our best," says personnel director Peter Russell, "to run a good school."

Who exactly, are the foreign teachers? Each year, the Immigration Bureau issues some 2,000 work visas to them. In reality, however, the rush to teach is much more dramatic. According to some of the schools themselves, 70,000 foreigners are teaching English at any given time in Tokyo alone, often on tourist visas. They are usually young people who have never taught before, but who find jobs quickly. This supports an irony: that in their enthusiasm to make English their second language, tens of thousands of Japanese are allowing themselves to be taught by unqualified people who happen to merely look or sound good.

One such tutor is a 20-year-old English-born truck driver. He is teaching at a large conversation school in Ikebukuro. "I get in there and do my thing," he says. "The students are happy." Another teacher was a carpet store manager in Oregon. "I don't teach language," he says. "Japanese hire me by the hour to talk to them."

"Yes," says Tracy Hartwick, also of JALT, and an instructor at Tokyo Foreign Language College, "the conversation schools hire anybody. They take foreigners virtually off the streets, so long as the manager is reasonably convinced that they have degrees." In many cases, of course, the "teachers" have no degrees, and the schools could not care less, particularly at a time when teachers are needed in a hurry.

Some instructors at nearly all the larger conversation schools have never been near a university in their lives. But Aki Fisher of Bi-Lingual's PR department, told me, "We have a very good training session." She later phoned back, however, to say that she had spoken to her bosses at Bi-Lingual, and that — according to the traditions of Japanese journalism — they require 21 days' notice about the kind of information an article concerning their company will contain before deciding whether or not they should "participate" in it. Further, they added, Bi-Lingual only hires university graduates. "But they don't," says another teacher who works there. "That's why the place is so bad."

Admittedly, some amateur teachers are conscientious, hard-working people who came to Japan to seek diversity and a change from a profession they followed at home — law, perhaps, accounting, or journalism — and who take an abundance of useful experience wherever they go. But quite often, the amateur teacher is merely a young "backpacker" who has arrived in Tokyo to make quick money, and who has joined a conversation school because a college won't hire him. He, or she, usually does have a degree, but if not, there are enough people who will gladly provide a fake one for the going rate of ¥6,000. According to his business card, one man who produced these holds an M.A., though he admits to dropping out of school, in Manchester, England, when he was 15. He is the coordinator of "student enrichment" at a so-called university near Shinjuku.

Sometimes, conversation schools are actually lucky to find professional teachers. When they do, though, it is usually because the teachers want to work for an employer who will sponsor them. Then once they have been granted working visas, they are often seen gleaning Monday's classified ads in *The Japan Times* in search of a job that calls for higher standards, and which offers about ¥100,000 a month more than the average ¥250,000 — or ¥2,800 an hour — that conversation schools generally pay their teachers.

By far the largest part of the problem is that too many schools are owned by Japanese entrepreneurs who liken their business to churning out doughnuts or sausages, or to fixing pipes. In it solely for the money, they don't even know — or care, come to that — that the foreigners they hire to run their schools, and teach in them, aren't qualified. They wouldn't know a college diploma or a university degree if they saw one. Nor would they know what a transcript was. They are the same people who, still meeting those student demands and bowing to shallow public sentiment, inject racism and all manner of discrimination into language teaching.

They do this in two ways.

First, they tend to employ only young people. Second, they perpetuate the myth that the best English is spoken in America, when, in fact, it is spoken by educated people in all corners of the English-speaking world. These are the same people who advertise for "American accents only," or for "blonde females under 29."

Experienced teachers who have moved from the conversation schools into the more structured field of English language education are also appalled by the amount of plagiarism the rush to learn English has created. Catherine Tansey, who has spent many of her 20 years in the education field editing, publishing, and selling textbooks for two American publishers, says, "It is extremely disquieting, not to mention unprofessional, to see that a lot of these conversation schools are compiling their texts from others that have already been properly published."

Nor are documents sacred. Ask Coral Harris about that. She noticed that the student evaluation form her Executive Education compiled when it first opened 17 years ago, was, until recently, being used by Interac. She knew it was hers because the typo she admits to creating was still there for all to see and smile at.

So the problem intensifies. But all is not lost. In June, a law was passed making it mandatory for Westerners to show the originals of their university degrees when applying for working visas — not just photocopies. Without this evidence of a university education, the visa will be denied. This, of course, is too bad for those people who want to drive trucks here, or do other jobs for which a degree is not necessary; it does, however, mean that those who want to teach English will, for the most part, be able to speak English reasonably well, and write it.

Another solution has evolved spontaneously: the conversation bar. No one, of course, pretends that conversation bars are great learning institutions, and neither do they purport to be. But then, neither is Bi-Lingual, ASA, Nova, or Plady House, which employs about 100 teachers. "We do our best to get experienced people," says Plady's PR director Hiryuki Okajima, "We look for people with a good degree."

A good degree? What is a good degree?

"English literature," says Okajima, "or something like it."

In truth, however, according to conversations with the instructors at Plady House, few have either "good degrees" or teaching experience. The conversation bars, meanwhile, are meeting the needs of those among Tokyo's "trendy" Japanese who want to mix with foreigners because it is the fashionable thing to do. And, unlike the schools, the bars are going about it unpretentiously and inoffensively, and without charging big money. One, for instance — Mickey House, in Takadanobaba — admits foreigners free and asks its

Japanese customers, mostly salarymen and women office workers, to pay a token ¥600 at the door. Coffee and tea are free, and so are the customers — to talk to whoever they wish, and for as long as they choose. In so doing, they may expose themselves to a collage of accents and backgrounds at an affordable price. And, by the way, beer is only ¥400 a glass!

"Meanwhile," says Catherine Tansey, "the more the Japanese people can get to know about language therapy and what creates success in it — whether they be language school managers or the students themselves — the better will be the choice of the appropriate institutions." Better schools and teachers, she adds, will automatically point students in the right direction — what course plan to follow, what realistic goals to pursue, what books to use and how, and what schools to attend. The people who are qualified to do this are not only people who know and speak English well, but those who have learned how to teach it.

Coral Harris agrees. "If the Japanese are really serious about learning English," she says, "they must recognize those schools that have rigidly high standards and stop opting for those that don't — the easy ones." These are the schools in which students are not expected to work hard because no one else, especially teachers, will do so on their behalf.

"If the teachers don't appreciate the difference between glamor and grammar," says Harris, "who will?"

A simple truth, a new friend

March 7, 1992

WHEN GIKON TAMAKI invites my wife and I for dinner, or is invited to our home for dinner, it is inevitably a unique occasion. I call Gikon the nail that sticks up, and who, according to all the traditions of Japanese society, should be hammered down. My wife says he's a Japanese original who seems to collect other Japanese originals. Thus, when we are together, the conversation runs fast and furious and touches, in some depth, on many topics.

In Totsuka the other night, for instance, in a restaurant called Ido, where Gikon had reserved a private table, we dealt with almost everything from Tokyo land prices, the cost of living, and the crumbling West, to American cars, my work, Gikon's work as a management consultant who gives seminars to sales personnel, and, of course, World War II and the events that sparked it.

Actually, I didn't bring this topic up at all. During the evening, several of Gikon's friends stopped by, one after the other, to meet us, and one of *them* raised it. I simply made the very general observation that the Japanese people of today were completely different from those who went to war with China in 1894 and Russia in 1904, invaded Manchuria in 1931, and who bombed Pearl Harbor in 1941. And to this, a woman, named Yoshiko Aoyagi, a teacher, said, "Oh yes, and that's because education is different now. The Japanese are no longer taught that they're invincible and that they should try to copy the British and the Dutch and have an empire."

Gikon, who knows how to keep a conversation light, or redirect it, declared, "I will drink to that!" He downed his *jokki* of black beer, and asked, "Anyone for second helpings?"

A wiry, compact man of 52, with sharp features and twinkling eyes, Gikon is a Japanese original because he is an incessant joker and is completely unafraid to express himself freely, as he thinks, not as he's been told to think — and in the courageous English he learned from language lessons on NHK-TV. Until then, I thought these lessons were useless, but Gikon Tamaki is walking testimony to the contrary.

Long after everyone else had finished their meal, he was still nibbling half-heartedly on a plate of what he called "ulcers."

"Ulcers?" I inquired, whereupon he consulted the English-Japanese dictionary he always carries with him.

"No, no, excuse me," he said, quickly. "Please make that oysters."

I first met Gikon when he invited my wife and I to watch him perform Japanese archery in Yokohama. He also pitched for a Totsuka old-timers' baseball team. In his last game, in December, he went three innings and gave up only one hit, but no walks. "I was an ace starting pitcher," he remembers, now peeling the shell from a giant prawn almost the size of a small chicken. "I was the greatest pitcher they ever had."

One of those friends who had come in from the cold

was stocky, gray-haired Masahiro Sekiguchi, a salesman for KLM and the team's former catcher and manager. "Saint Masa," as he is known because he "has no faults," was one of the best listeners I'd ever encountered, only ever answering a question when one was put directly to him.

"Was Gikon Tamaki really a star pitcher?"

"No, I don't think so," said Saint Masa, straight-faced. Then, heaving with loud laughter, he added, "He was very bad!"

Gikon also joked that he had recently been scouted by the Hiroshima Carp, his favorite team, but hastily conceded, "OK, so I was a bad pitcher. But that was in December. I've improved since then."

His emotional ties to the Carp, by the way, seem logical. He was born in 1939, in Totsukawa, a small village on Hiroshima's outskirts, and grew up in nearby Itsukaichi, about 20 km from where the A-bomb would have struck the ground had it not been designed to explode above it. He faintly remembers the flash of white light that silenced a great city, and the surge of hot air that blasted in the windows of his parents' home.

Masahiro Sekiguchi recalls that his three older brothers served with the Japanese army overseas, and that one never came home because he had starved to death in New Guinea.

It was just before midnight when the restaurant staff asked Gikon if his guests wanted any more black beer, and it was then that Saint Masa sidled toward me across the tatami.

"You and your wife," he observed, his narrowing eyes filling with tears, "are the first foreigners I have ever heard distinguish between the Japanese of today and those of forty to fifty years ago. Thank you very much. That's all I want to say. Thank you very much."

By saying something I and a lot of other foreigners honestly thought, I had made another friend.

Gikon broke the tension. "Regretfully, very regretfully, this is the last call for second helpings," he said, raising his empty beer glass. "Let's drink to staying in touch with each other."

Ah! What lurks behind language!

January 18, 1992

EVERY SATURDAY MORNING — with a kiss and a smile, and as early as possible — my wife sends me out of the apartment. I joke too much, she says, and she's probably right. My propensity for joking is as legendary as my fear of snakes, my love of socks, and my lust for exploration, which brings me to my point. When set loose on Saturdays, I invariably hunt out those places that have hidden for far too long behind the crowds in narrow streets, and, of course, the language barrier. They are there all right. But where, exactly?

Some while ago, I lost a brass blazer button. Actually, I saw it on the railway carriage floor, but couldn't find the space to bend down to recover it. Someone then kicked it onto a platform, and someone else kicked it under the train. So, I had to search for another button.

At one department store, the clerk wanted to sell me a complete set of them — 10 for ¥6,000! "Are you crazy?" I said. "The jacket didn't cost much more than that!" When I asked her, and several other clerks, to direct me to a button shop, she couldn't.

Not to worry. The other day, not too far from the Totsuka Ward Office, and about 50 steps from my bank, I found what I wanted — a shop that had brass buttons everywhere you looked. The woman who, for a modest ¥120, sold me one that matched all the others on my blazer, even looked like a brass button.

I also found my barber nearby, which was another help. When we lived in a foreigners' house in Iogi last year, the men there came upon a man who cut hair for ¥1,700. One day, we sent the landlord to him and he returned somewhat perturbed because he was charged ¥2,800! Why? The ¥1,700 was a special price for foreigners, the barber told him. Since Japanese men had more and thicker hair, servicing them took longer and was therefore worth more money.

Can you believe it? It's true — about the landlord, I mean. Anyway, my last haircut cost ¥3,800 — a little expensive, I thought, because I no longer have that much hair. Not far from the Totsuka button shop, however, conveniently near a Doutor coffee shop, is a barber who charges only ¥2,100. And, of almost equal significance is that nearby, several shops sell discounted liquor. In fact, crates of whiskeys, brandies, and gins seem to overflow onto the sidewalk, where I have bought good scotch for as little as ¥2,000 a bottle.

That's not all. The other day, I spent nearly two hours looking for pipe tobacco. When I asked for the tobacco center in Marui, a clerk said, "Over there." I went over there, but returned baffled. Her colleague then said, "Please go over there," and pointed in the same direction. I then found two machines, both packed tightly with cigarettes. But neither had pipe tobacco.

These damned machines are the scourge of my life! I hate them. One day, one is sure to confiscate my Fuji Bank card, and a woman's recorded voice will say, politely of course, "Ha! Now try and get it back." I know it will happen, but not in Totsuka. I have faith in small places. I eventually found a kiosk sandwiched between a pawnbroker's establishment and a hardware shop that has a reasonable stock of pipe tobaccos, except my brand wasn't there, and the owner couldn't understand what it was I wanted. So I may have to smoke something different for a while.

Totsuka also has a store called Uny, where almost everything is cheaper than it is in others of its kind. Like the shop I told you about in Shibuya, it sells inexpensive CDs.

Oh, I almost forgot. Because that Doutor coffee shop actually fills up the cup to the brim, it means I don't have to ask for hot water to be added, like I do elsewhere. But, I suppose, you can't have everything in life, can you?

A few weeks ago, some Japanese friends took my wife and me to dinner in a place opposite Uny. We ended up in a buffet-style Japanese restaurant where you can actually see what you want to eat before ordering it, so nothing is ever a surprise. Three meat or fish dishes, a bowl of rice, a bowl of hot miso soup, and a bottomless cup of green tea, costs ¥800 at lunch time, and not much more at dinner time. The restaurant sells something else I have been searching for, too — black beer!

What else can a man want? Everything I ever sought is right there, in one little corner of dusty Totsuka. Or *almost* everything. I have yet to see a shop that repairs IBM computer keyboards, however, though I'm sure one will come, if it isn't already there — lurking in a narrow street, behind the crowds and vegetable stalls, and, of course, the language barrier.

The stuff of dreams

March 28, 1992

WE WERE IN KYOTO, Japan's most beautiful city, I seem to recall — my wife Irene, daughter Nathalie, and me — and had been given some sort of coupon as a promotional ploy. Whenever we showed it while using a Visa card, we stood a chance of winning a prize; the more money we charged, the greater that prize would be. Predictably, for she is still a child, Nathalie kept pestering me to give her the coupon — and my Visa card — so she could buy strawberry-flavored chewing gum, or something else just as trivial. I constantly refused, maintaining that if we waited until I bought a more expensive item, like a jacket or a big bottle of perfume, we would stand a much bigger chance of both hitting the jackpot and winning a lot of money.

Well, the big moment came, and the three of us trooped into a large department store, where I bought a coat. And, sure enough, I was lucky! As the card was inserted into it, the cash register convulsed, rocked, squeaked, and sang a happy song. And the smiling woman clerk said, in Japanese, of course, "Congratulations, Sir! You have just won fifty-two-thousand American dollars!"

God knows why my winnings were in dollars and not in yen. Anyway, just as the clerk was about to hand me the money in a big, brown envelope, I felt a hand on my shoulder, gently rocking me back and forth.

35

"Turn on your side," Irene said. "You're snoring — again."

It had all been another stupid dream.

Even so, I lay awake for some time — quite disappointed that I didn't get the money and annoyed that I should have been awakened at such an inopportune time. I didn't even get to touch the envelope!

Eventually, I got up, made a cup of coffee, went back to bed, fell asleep quickly, then promptly started to dream again. This time, I dreamed there was a squirrel in the park opposite our apartment, and a large serpent. (My fear of snakes, by the way, is very real and stretches back to my short stint as a British soldier on active service in Malaysia.) The squirrel, I recall now, was dead, with blood on its nose, and the serpent was so much alive that when I tried to strike it with the broom I use to sweep the balcony, it reared up and winked at me.

The more I tried to fell it with one healthy swipe, the more the serpent seemed to enjoy itself. Finally, as I aimed a gun at it, it smiled more widely than ever. And just as I was about to pull the trigger, the alarm went off and I had to start another work day, battling bodies on the trains and fretting because I never get a seat. I was so disturbed about all this dreaming that I couldn't wait to get to the office to share it with someone.

I haven't been sleeping at all well lately, and when I tell myself I will, I invariably enter into shallow slumber because of a series of the most preposterous dreams imaginable, all of them totally illogical in content, and all of them foreign to my nature.

One night, for instance, I woke up laughing —

uncontrollably. I enjoyed that, though. Laughter is a wonderful thing, especially when you can share it with someone. But you can't wake someone up in the middle of the night and say, "Hey, d'you want to hear a joke or a funny experience?" That doesn't go down too well.

On this particular occasion, however, I didn't for the life of me know what was so funny. I had absolutely no recollection of anything amusing of note, except the sight of little Prime Minister Miyazawa standing next to lanky George Bush — the long and the short of it. I'm not given much to laughing at nothing. So, once again, I got up and made myself a cup of coffee, and, sitting in the living room, remembered other ridiculous dreams I'd had — like the one terminated abruptly when, while living in that foreigners' house in Iogi, I rolled from my futon.

I was dreaming then that when I arrived in Shinjuku on my way to work one morning, I could read every Japanese billboard I saw! More than that, when I arrived in the office, people there said I actually looked Japanese, and this made me happy because — at last — I felt one of the crowd instead of just an outsider.

Perhaps that reflects a truth: that I have spent the last 20 years of my life in parts of the world in which I have been a member of various minority groups — in Quebec, the French-speaking province of Canada, in Florida, where I have another home, and, of course, in Japan, where laws persist in making me, and a lot of other people, feel an outsider, even though I pay my share of income tax and ward tax, and contribute to a company pension plan from which I can never hope to draw.

But I still can't fathom the significance of winning $52,000 in Kyoto, or trying to fell a serpent. One night, with luck, I will tune into those dreams again — just to garner a greater understanding of what is going on. If I do, I will update you.

I RECEIVED A LETTER from Gikon Tamaki this week. Remember him? He's the jovial fellow of 52 — a real Japanese original, my wife calls him — who says that until December, he was the "star pitcher" of a Totsuka old timers' baseball team. Gikon is a lot more than this, of course — a management consultant who gives seminars to sales personnel, a studious archer, and a zealous custodian of Japanese tradition.

He acquired his courageous English, by the way, by watching language lessons on NHK-TV, and taking copious notes on how to use verbs and idioms to speak eloquently about his passion for life and how he refuses to take himself too seriously.

On this latter point. Gikon once said that if he worked for a Japanese company, instead of for himself, he would have to watch the way others perceived him. For the moment, though, he doesn't. And that's what I like about him.

> *Hi! This is the nail that should be hammered down — your friend Gikon. Ha! Ha! I'm in Atami, where there is a seminar house of my main client company. Regretfully — and regretfully — there are no geisha girls by my side, because I'm here on business. Ha! Ha!*
>
> *I apologize to you for being late with this. In fact, I had been very busy until yesterday making the documents for my*

final income tax return of this fiscal year. Preparing the documents is always a conflict between my conscience, which says I have to pay as much income tax as possible as a Japanese national, and my defiant feeling that I don't want to contribute to scandalous politicians and the obstinate and inefficient public sector, and so forth. Ha!

I read your column of March 7 and am glad to see that I appeared in it because I'll become a well-known person among foreign people living in Japan, and I might be scouted even by the Cincinnati Reds. Ha! Ha!

The Reds is one of my favorite American baseball teams because their uniforms are almost the same as the Hiroshima Carp.

Anyway, I deeply appreciated seeing my name in your column. You gave me appropriate (even exaggerated) recognition. You really have a watchful eye. Ha! Ha! Ha!

Well, I have to close this now.

See you later! Cheers!

Gikon Tamaki.

Thank you, Gikon. Keep reading.

Yasushi's yen for honesty
March 14, 1992

NOT LONG AGO, JUST A FEW weeks before his ninth birth-day, Yasushi Ebizuka had an urgent appointment at the Totsuka district police headquarters — urgent for him, that is — in connection with something that happened last summer. While playing outside a convenience store in neighboring Higashi-Totsuka, he found some money on the sidewalk and was suddenly on fire with all that he had been taught by his parents and school teachers alike, an important component in the preservation of Japan's group harmony.

If ever anyone finds anything that is so obviously lost, no matter how large or small it may be, he or she must hand it to the authorities so that the rightful owner may get it back. Such is the unwritten creed of Japan, and we are all so grateful for it.

So, with his little heart pounding with discovery and sudden fortune, Yasushi took the money to the local police station where an officer sat him on a chair, reached for a form, and spent several minutes filling it in, finally adorning it with the police department's *hanko*. It was an official document, indeed, and it was with this that Yasushi raced home to tell his mother what he had done.

After six months, the form said, Yasushi could call the cash his very own, and it would be waiting for him at district headquarters — but only if it remained unclaimed. It doubtless was, for Yasushi Ebizuka had found, and handed in, ¥1!

Now, though, he had to face reality, which his mother was quick to point out. To collect his ¥1, he would have to take a ¥70 train trip to Totsuka, then a ¥100 bus ride to police headquarters. Yasushi was unmoved. He always wanted to see the inside of such a busy building, anyway.

Conveniently, his mother, Eiko Ebizuka, forgot about the ¥1, and the deadline for collecting it came and went. But the story does not end here. A few weeks after plucking the coin from the sidewalk, luck was on Yasushi's side once more — this time while making his daily rounds of the neighborhood, and daydreaming as he went. When he found a crumpled ¥5,000 note near an apartment building's garbage bins, guess what he did with it!

Right! Without even thinking of putting the money in his pocket and telling no one about it, he took it back to the same police station where the same police-man drew another form from his desk drawer, filled it in, applied the hanko, and handed it to him to take home.

This time, Yasushi's thoughts — for the most part cluttered with dreams of yogurt-flavored chewing gum, baseball, comic strips, and frogs — were overtaken by something else. If the rightful owner did not claim this money — and who on this earth could possibly say that a ¥5,000 note found by a garbage bin was truly his? — he would at last own big, very big money.

How big? To listen to the boy, he was about to inherit an absolute fortune that was 50 times the monthly allowance his father, Professor Yutaka Ebizuka of the University of Tokyo's department of pharmaceutical sciences, gives him for washing the odd dish and helping his mother clean. It was the kind of money that would buy him some of the things he has dreamed of: a Game Boy, perhaps, a calculator, or a plastic baseball bat.

Unwittingly, however, this was only part of the deal. At least, that's how I see it. From the moment they have learned the difference between right and wrong, most children are honest. If they are ever to be dishonest, they will surely learn it from other, older people. The police know this, of course, and that is why they rewarded Yasushi in another way. For handing in the ¥1 on that bright summer's afternoon, his name was added to a list of other boys and girls who had been good that month and published it in a newsletter circulated by the local police box. Skeptics might say that this was what may have fired Yasushi's imagination in the first place — the chance of publicity. After all, that ¥1 bought him a lot of public relations and prestige. It also earned him a lot of personal honor. Just imagine Yasushi Ebizuka being mentioned in a circular that is read by thousands of people!

But even that was far from his mind. According to his mother, he never even knew that the newsletter existed, nor the Totsuka police headquarters, come to that. Nonetheless, and not long ago, she and Yasushi went there to collect the ¥5,000. Of this, her son has since spent ¥1,200 — on two comic books and a set of playing cards. And, oh yes, he insisted that now he was finally "in the money," so to speak, he would reimburse her for his rail and bus fares to pick it up, which is exactly what he did.

What now of the future? Are any investments planned? As he shuffles his cards with two open comic books nearby, Yasushi Ebizuka stares at the table and says, "I am too shy to talk about it."

Loudness condescends

April 28, 1990

THERE IS, I THINK, a disturbing trait among too many Westerners. When speaking to the Japanese, they raise their voices so as to put themselves in a dominant position. Yet all they ever really need to do is be is themselves. Not that they always mean to be condescending. They don't. The fact is, though, that when addressing their Japanese friends loudly — and in pidgin English to boot — they are inadvertently relegating them to a lower plane, and, as we know so well, the Japanese are far too proud and polite a people to protest.

Let's consider some analogies.

Doctors like to be in a dominant position and often think they need to be if they are to be effective. Perhaps that is why, when you are lying helplessly in hospital, the physician or surgeon in charge of that day's rounds of the wards, moors himself at the foot of your bed then, looking down at you, inquires, "How is the patient today? Is he feeling better?"

The doctor invariably does this in an exceedingly loud voice as if to imply that between you and him there must be no secrets. In so doing, everyone else in the ward, or even in the next, hears exactly what he is asking, even if they preferred not to.

I get annoyed with my dental hygienist. "Oh," she says in a voice that echoes far beyond the area of the chair, "you're not smoking as much, and you've cut down on coffee. But you must floss a little more." She speaks to me just as she would a little boy, and probably doesn't know she does it.

Then there is the way we tend to speak to the infirm or the blind.

I know a man so inflicted who spends his days in a shopping mall in my home town of Montreal, just so he can be with people. If you were blind like him, the skin on your left forefinger would be tough from guiding a lighter onto each new cigarette, and your hand would be moving all the time across the table top checking, remembering — glass, ashtray, cigarettes. And, I think, you'd find that world of the sighted is a very thoughtless place, with parking meters set just far enough from the curb to catch you in the stomach when you felt your way home with a white stick. The noise of the traffic would leave you helpless, and you'd have to tell a man by the quality of his voice because long ago, you would have given up trying to visualize how people looked, and they'd just be meaningless shadows, anyway.

And if you were very blind, you'd always be fighting this lingering, nibbling sense of inferiority which would not be helped by the way people spoke to you. In restaurants, you'd know the waitresses always wanted to help out by the way they scurried about earnestly to make you comfortable. But if you were blind, you'd also quickly discover that they'd reduce you to a third person, and somewhat of a second-class citizen, by addressing the man or woman with you — "Does your friend take cream in his coffee? Does she like her eggs over and easy?"

Worse, you'd have to damn well get used to the way nearly all people raised their voices when they spoke to you, as if being blind meant you were half deaf or half daft, too.

So it is that all too many of us Westerners address the Japanese. We are generally taller than they are, and, with relatively few exceptions, we expect them to speak our language. We do no service whatsoever by treating them as anything but equals — no matter how their culture and traditions have established the way they must perceive us.

I have no pat answers to the questions of just how we might best communicate with the Japanese, except to suggest that they deserve to be addressed in the same way that we would address anyone in our own country. Pidgin English should be replaced by simple, standard English that is uncluttered by slang, lightened by a lack of idiom that may not cross ethnic borders, delivered slowly and clearly, and repeated as many times as may be necessary — in a normal voice — for them to understand.

Blueprint for prosperity

February 9, 1991

THE LITTLE PREFECTURE of Oita has always been pro-
gressive. Fortitude, resilience, and imagination are
somehow etched in the hearts and minds of its 1.25
million people.

Back in the 16th century, it was the seat of Otomo
Sorin, a Christian feudal lord who viewed the world —
and wanted it. He traded with the Portuguese, imported
Western music, theater, schools, and hospitals, and
invited Chinese missionaries. For all this, and over long
years, the prefecture remained relatively poor, relying
mostly on agriculture, fishing, and what tourism it could
attract. By the beginning of the century, most of its
young people had begun to move away to larger centers
like Tokyo and Osaka in search of jobs and fortune.

Today, though, things are different there. Oita,
largely mountainous, is governed by a corpulent, free-
smiling man named Morihiko Hiramatsu, 62, who
believes in "borderless economies," the decentralization
of government, regional pride, and "people power."
When he took office in 1979, he told himself that his
prefecture was indeed depressed, but that it had a lot
to sell. "Think globally, but act locally," he declared.

Heavy industry had thrived there for some years —
principally oil refining, pulp, and food processing.
Additionally, Nippon Steel had a plant near Oita City,
as did the petrochemical firm, Showa Denko. But, for

Hiramatsu, who was born in Oita City and grew up there, they did not employ nearly enough people or inspire them to stay. His idea, to stabilize the local economy and bring former residents scurrying back, was by attracting an array of new industries, and developing some of Oita's indigenous products as they had never been developed before.

Principal crops grown on level areas of the prefecture, mostly strewn along its 746 km of coastline against the Inland Sea, had always been rice, mandarin oranges, and vegetables. Forestry on the mountainsides, and cattle breeding and fishing elsewhere, were — and still are — important sources of income, too. But Hiramatsu felt they could be more so.

So, in an orgy of inspiration — and with a motto: "Let's Love Oita" — he began to turn things around. He launched his "One Village, One Product" campaign to inspire each prefectural community to take pride in producing local specialties so well that they could be ushered into domestic and world markets. Towns and villages that grew fruit were inspired to produce by-products — juice, jam, and spreads. Fishing centers were encouraged to make fish paste, soups, and chowders. And many communities that had no local specialties at all were taught how to develop them. Hence, Oita now produces everything from mushrooms, bungo beef, prawns, limes, and pickles, to sardines, bamboo crafts, plums, furniture, and pearls.

And industry? As shipyards and coal mines closed, Japan's southern-most island attracted many electronics and computer software manufacturers. Predictably, some of them ended up in Oita, thus dubbing it "Silicon City."

The economic results of Hiramatsu's vision have been staggering, indeed. In less than a decade, the prefecture's unemployment rate has dropped from 10 percent to less than two percent, and its population has stabilized for the first time in 100 years. And although in terms of industrial strength it is middling among Japan's 47 prefectures, the presidents of 1,053 corporations listed on the First Section of the Tokyo Stock Exchange have ranked Oita second only to Tokyo in economic, cultural, and political vitality.

More important to Oita's 370,000 households is that in terms of quality of life, it is now 28th in Japan as compared to 47th 10 years ago. This is because its annual per capita income has increased over the same period from ¥1.6 million to nearly ¥2 million. Once at the bottom of Japan's prefectures in terms of earning power, it is now 27th — and is climbing.

Nothing better explains why news of Oita's success has spread across the world. Two years ago, Louisiana's governor, Buddy Roemer, went there to see intelligent economic development at its best so he could implement it back home. "I want to see," he said, "what product, parish-by-parish, can be grown, sold, or traded in Louisiana." Cities like Shanghai and Wuhan in China, and Languedoc-Roussillon in southern France, have also embraced the idea, and last year, Los Angeles Mayor Tom Bradley declared October 6 "One Village, One Product Day"— to recognize Hiramatsu's work. Hiramatsu, however, was too busy working to attend the ceremony. "I had several meetings that day," he says. "You have to keep ahead of things."

Morihiko Hiramatsu was born in Oita City in March 1924, the son of a hatter. Actually, his father was originally a school teacher, turning to making hats when he inherited the business of his wife's grandfather. When it folded at the outset of World War II, he returned to education. In fact, one of his greatest contributions to Oita, besides sitting on the Oita City Council, was a school he had established in 1925, to give ordinary people an education at night.

Now, each of Oita's 12 regions still has a similar school with similar aims — to teach local people such professions as accounting, word processing, even law — and Governor Hiramatsu heads all of them.

He had a good education himself. After graduating from Oita Middle School, he entered Kumamoto High School, now Kumamoto University. His studies were interrupted, however, when he was called into the Imperial Navy at the outset of World War II. He served as a naval accountant, reached the rank of lieutenant, but spent most of his service pawing over ledgers on board a ship docked near Kure. In 1946, when he left the navy, he entered the Tokyo University Law School, graduating five years later.

Instead of entering private practice, Hiramatsu joined the Ministry of International Trade and Industry (MITI), where he headed the Heavy Industry Bureau's Electronics Industry Division. He was an early believer in the importance of using computers to gather and store information for industrial and social development. In fact, partly as a hobby, he is a member of the local computer club, which has hook-ups via modems to such far-flung places as Seoul and Santa Monica. The club also gathers requests and complaints from residents. "Computers," says the governor, "help me listen to the people."

While he was on leave from MITI, to serve as a councilor in the National Land Agency's Secretariat, the then Oita governor, Masaru Taki, urged him to return to his home prefecture to be its deputy governor. Hiramatsu did, and nearly four years later he was elected governor. It was the beginning of three successive terms in which he has received overwhelming support at the polls. In the last election, for instance, he garnered more than 612,000 votes — an astonishing 84.3 percent of the popular vote — and his only opposition came from a member of the Japan Communist Party who thought Hiramatsu was ushering the prefecture along the road to ruin.

Capitalism, however, was what the people of Oita wanted, and it came from the heart and the hip of Morihiko Hiramatsu. And the transformation of the prefecture, which had begun two elections before, continued.

Looking back, the governor says, he was fueled by three things. First came the "energy and the can-do spirit" of his father whose motto was "Perseverance is Power." Second, there was his work with MITI, which enabled him to learn the enormous potential of a computerized world. Third, he has always cited the ingenuity and resilience of his father-in-law, Tamotsu Ueda, who, for 14 years, was Oita City's mayor.

One story goes that back in the 1950s, when farmers complained bitterly that monkeys on Mount Takasaki were destroying their crops, Mayor Ueda stumbled upon an ingenious idea. Instead of exterminating the animals, as many people wanted the city to do, he advocated feeding them. This way, he maintained, the monkeys would cease being a local nuisance and become a tourist attraction instead. Not only that, it was the kind and honorable thing to do. Now, almost 40 years later, Monkey Mountain, with its 1,700 wild inhabitants, is one of the first places in Oita that visitors clamor to see.

Says Hiramatsu, "This kind of philosophy, to do what's right, and persevere by turning something negative into something positive — even in the face of stern opposition — is what Oita is all about in 1991. I can thank my father-in-law for showing me that, in action."

There was little opposition, however, when, from the very day he occupied his new, spacious office overlooking sprawling Oita City, he began to actively promote economic progress in local areas with his "One Village, One Product" campaign. The concept, then unique, was put forth to encourage local areas to create and market products special to their respective localities — plums, initially, then apples, and prawns. "The idea is based on the philosophy of self-reliance, and depends on the energy, creativity, and will of the local citizens using local resources to enhance their economic well-being," Hiramatsu says. "It is far more productive and dignified than dishing out local subsidies."

At the back of his mind was a startling revelation: that the exodus from his prefecture had left behind a population that was ageing between 10 and 15 years faster than those in other areas of Japan. This, he says, was why, at Beppu, a coastal town about 20 km from Oita City, where about 50 percent of Japan's bambooware is produced, he established his New Life Plaza. Here, the elderly learn such skills as computer programming and basket making so they will not be left out of the prefecture's on-going economic miracle.

"We must breathe new life into our ageing society," Hiramatsu says. And he adds, "The important thing is that instead of giving subsidies to local areas, which, in other parts of the country often result in the decline of the spirit of self-reliance, we encouraged each community by providing technical assistance for the improvement of the quality of the product, and assistance to both publicize and market it."

Indeed, he was so bent on seeing that Oita's products were good enough for wide distribution, that he set up the prefecture's Agricultural and Marine Product Processing Research and Information Center — the first of its kind to be established by a local government anywhere in Japan. Here, farmers and fishermen learn how to develop by-products from their produce, process and package them, then sell them as far afield as they can.

First, though, produce must be developed or grown. Heat from several of Oita's 4,223 hot springs is being used to simulate a tropical climate in which experienced gardeners can grow roses, chrysanthemums, and orchids — all year round! Some steam-heated green houses also produce vegetables. Meanwhile, computerized fish-feeding grounds have been built. One of them, Marine Ranch, the first of its kind in the world, employs a unique sonar system. The sonar sends out a certain pitch to new-born red sea bream while they are being fed, and they come to associate the sound with the pleasures of eating.

As the fish mature, they learn to respond to the signal for feeding, thus facilitating fish management and harvesting. Says Hiramatsu, "The advanced technology of our area has a big role to play in our vision."

It has. Through it, together with the constant efforts of most of Oita's communities, other new products like shochu, sake, and wine have emerged — in addition to the already world-famous *shiitake* mushrooms. To improve the taste of local tangerines, Hiramatsu singlehandedly persuaded bio-engineers to create a special Oita citrus through cross-fertilization with U.S. navel oranges. And, thanks to his encouragement, and the marketing facilities he put at their disposal, the prawn farmers of Himeshima Island made a profit of ¥50 billion last year alone.

Morihiko Hiramatsu's ultimate goal, after all, is to harness, foster, and refine Oita's human resources as best he can. To this end, his prefecture has also provided an educational training school called the Toyonokuni-zukuri Juku, where young leaders learn how to "build a more affluent society," so they may tread in their governor's footsteps.

Unquestionably, however, most of Oita's new-found affluence has been derived from the new industry it has drawn under a program called Technopolis. While the prefecture's Greenopolis project aims to revitalize leading lumber areas on the one hand, and preserve parks and nature areas on the other, Technopolis is concerned only with building a tax base through business.

Basically, Technopolis is an extension of Hiramatsu's original theory — that certain businesses flourish best near a major airport. With this in mind, he earmarked certain land for industrial development within a 50-km radius of Oita Airport — built on a man-made peninsular in Oita Bay — and watched dozens of Japanese firms develop there and thrive. Predictably, most are electronic, mechatronic, and high-tech companies that need to be close to an airport anyway, so they can ship their goods and receive spare parts quickly.

In recent years, industrial expansion has spread throughout the prefecture, though it has been contained to five specific areas, one of which is Soft Park, a little empire of software developers and academic advisors. "The task," says Hiramatsu, "is to integrate high-tech industries, transportation systems, academic research facilities, and urban facilities into a meaningful entity so that they feed from each other and thrive side by side."

At the latest count, Oita has 2,559 factories and 3,452 businesses, and about a third of them have opened there since 1979. "When I came here from MITI," Hiramatsu says, unabashedly, "I asked my friends to start companies in Oita, and they cooperated."

With another prefectural election in April, Governor

Hiramatsu is hoping that his friends will continue to support him at the polls, and that the public will not take his re-election too much for granted. Though popular in other parts of Japan, he is not without dissenters on his home turf. At an assembly meeting not long ago, for instance, an opponent said of him, "He's like the sunflower that always turns to the bright sun, remaining ignorant of his own shadow below."

Hiramatsu's reply was equally poetic. Referring to a local fruit known for being plentiful, and for having a beautiful flower, he replied, "I am the bungo plum that blossoms in the bitterest cold."

He is.

"I would say," he says, "that we've achieved about 80 percent of objectives for the first term, and the plan is progressing smoothly. But I've often said that what we need more than high-tech is 'lo-tech,' meaning local technology. We now have to develop our local grassroots technologies."

To help do it, the prefecture is also spending ¥100 million to upgrade its telecommunications system. It is also improving roads, railways, and shipping facilities to give it greater access than ever to the outside world. And this, says Hiramatsu, is something Tokyo has not done.

"If I were prime minister," Hiramatsu says, "I would move universities out of Tokyo to ease the congestion there. It must also be done to promote economic, technological, and human exchanges between local cities. This way, local cities can serve as regional intellectual centers, easing the information burden in Tokyo." And he adds, "Local cities can do better than Tokyo under what I call the Kyushu Government Plan.

Kyushu would have a comprehensive office to function as a representative of the central government, so it would be able to make all decisions on all matters related to the island itself. We would have a similar office in Sendai to cover the Tohoku area, and in Osaka to cover the Kansai area."

He is a man, says an admirer, who not only views the world like Otomo Sorin, that Christian feudal lord, but all of Japan. And he wants to see Oita become the heart and soul of it.

Of rice and men
April 11, 1992

Around the dinner table in Totsuka, Gikon and his
five friends discuss every major issue that has confronted
Japan during the past 10 years. Well, nearly every one.
Each agrees that the death penalty should remain the
ultimate punishment for murder. Each feels that not
enough foreigners take time to try to understand the
Japanese way of doing things, and that when it comes
to discussing their country, Americans appear hopelessly
ill-informed. There is nothing wrong with the people,
of course. Like Gikon, who has arranged the dinner,
they are gentle, well-mannered, and inscrutably honest
— typical Japanese, in fact, with what appear to be
typical views.

Would they buy an American car? All say no —
emphatically — because, they feel, they would not be
buying quality, and that parts might not be easy to get.
All also say they would not buy American cars even if
they were cheaper than Japanese cars, and no amount
of convincing them that Americans are, in fact, now
producing reasonably good small vehicles has much
effect. The minds around that table are firmly made up.

What about Japan opening its rice market to
imports, principally those from the United States? I like
American rice. I also like Japanese rice. The two are
completely different. Although I don't agree that this
should be the issue, I can understand those Japanese

who view rice as being at the very center of their culture — a sort of symbol of their struggle and their unity.

Gikon disagrees. "I don't see any cultural value in rice at all," he says, "but maybe that's because I live in the city." And he adds, "If by importing rice our farmers are affected financially, they must find something else to grow."

Many of them are already looking at such alternatives as plums, nuts, and mushrooms, having decided that the time when Japan allows American rice into the marketplace is not too far away.

But how do Japanese women view American rice? Without exception, all say they would be happy to try it, and if they liked it, they would buy it again. But they cannot promise to serve it regularly because, they have heard that whereas Japanese rice is soft and gooey, and can therefore be eaten with chopsticks, American rice tends to be dry, and therefore can't be. Two women say, "We need to make sushi and we don't think this could be done with any other rice but our own." So, by consensus, the women agreed that if and when American rice finds its way into Japan, they might only use it once in a while, and only for those meals, like curry, that can be eaten with a spoon.

How do the Japanese see themselves? That was a long, drawn-out topic that did not produce any startling revelations. My wife Irene says she likes the way the Japanese make verbal promises and keep them, to which Gikon explains, "That's because before the Meiji period, few people could write anyway. So a contract had to be verbal."

The women wonder if the Japanese really are as

honest as foreigners say they are. I tell them that this honesty among the "ordinary" people is what endears foreigners to Japan. Gikon then tells us that when the Japanese travel abroad, they do not hunt out bargains — cheap clothes, cheap meals, or cheap hotel rooms — like Westerners tend to do, because they are so used to paying high prices for virtually everything at home that the cost of living abroad usually fits their pocket books admirably.

At one point, I make another simple observation: that the Japanese are unique, completely unlike any other people I have ever met. This, I feel, is largely because whereas most other languages have a relative of some sort, Japanese doesn't. And, since language defines a culture, the Japanese have always banded together, and done things together and in the same way to protect it. Mainly through sharing a language that no one else speaks, it has been forced to become a group society.

"I don't do things the same way as other Japanese," one woman contends. "Maybe I am different." When I explain that the Japanese cross the road together, line up for trains the same way, learn English and speak it the same way, use the same mannerisms when they speak, she agrees that I am probably right, and says, "I never thought of it like that. Maybe we *are* all alike."

We speak about the Japanese family, and why each Japanese person at the dinner table, except for an unmarried woman of 20, is without his or her spouse. Each husband or wife has a different circle of friends, is the general reply, and each leads a fairly independent life anyway.

One thing we agree on is that whereas Japanese men have almost always put their working lives ahead of all other things, the time has now come for them to strengthen their family lives. "After all," I tell the gathered group, "friends come and go, but a family is made and should be kept together at all costs."

"I will drink to that," Gikon says.

ONTO OTHER THINGS not too far removed from what the people were saying at Gikon's dinner party. It was pretty obvious to a lot of us when President George Bush arrived in Tokyo to try to promote business and boost his chances of re-election, that the Japanese know far more about the United States than Americans know about Japan. I can't document the former, though my wife has been able to cast light upon the latter — by polling her 10 most-traveled students on how they think the Japanese are perceived by Americans. The results of that little survey are not profound, of course, but they are nonetheless revealing.

And laughable, I might add. Most Americans these students met during visits to such cities as Los Angeles, Chicago, and New York, tended to believe that:

- All Japanese are rich
- All Japanese women are housewives
- Most Japanese women are weak
- Many Japanese women are geisha
- The Japanese are arrogant
- The Japanese are belligerent and "love" war
- Japanese people wear masks because of the large amount of pollution in their cities

- All Japanese people are diligent and good at mathematics and science
- All Japanese people are good at karate, and other martial arts
- The Japanese cannot invent anything of their own, and only ever copy other people's ideas
- All Japanese people wear kimono
- Japanese people look the same as other Asians
- The Japanese do not buy American goods

More certain is that when George Bush receives Prime Minister Miyazawa, if both men are still in power, he will shake his hand warmly, and tell him, "This time, Kiichi, lunch is on me."

REMEMBER MY COLUMN "Yasushi's yen for honesty" about the nine-year-old boy whose conscience took hold of him so much when he found a ¥1 coin, that he handed it in at the local police box? Well, Yasushi's mother, Eiko Ebizuka, wrote to me this week. "Your column gave us great enjoyment," she said. "I showed it to Yasushi but, unfortunately, he couldn't read it because it was in English."

But she adds, "I will keep this edition of *The Japan Times Weekly* as a keepsake and show it to him when he is old enough to understand it. My husband and I are very proud that you wrote about Yasushi."

On singing like a thrush
December 21, 1991

YOU'D LIKE THE FOLKS down at my local electronics store in Higashi-Totsuka. I do. They all seem to amble about with permanent smiles, nod graciously, and, when you ask for something, give the general impression that nothing will ever be too much trouble. Except one man, that is. But then, one cold night, music brought us together.

Until then, he had been a pained, shy figure. True, he didn't speak English, but then, neither did his colleagues. When I stopped by for a film for my Handycam, he inevitably saw me coming, and, checking behind him, fled among the washing machines. If I sought a battery, you could bet your boots he'd head for the word processors, or the air conditioners. Once, when I wanted to check the price of an electric tooth brush, he appeared not to hear me and darted over to the refrigerators.

Our reconciliation happened like this:

Late one Sunday night not too long ago, I popped in for a heater. The shop was almost empty when I arrived, and all the television sets had been turned off, the CD players silenced. It was unusually quiet for such a busy place, save for a few last-minute customers — and the single sound of one man.

There, on a little podium near the doorway, stood our shy clerk, microphone in hand — singing! He was,

63

I believe, demonstrating a home *karaoke* device, an ingenious sort of invention that magnifies the voice through a radio receiver while simultaneously spreading the words of a song on a television screen. There you have it — all the ingredients for a karaoke session right in your living room, and this man, his chest swelling with pride, was proving that it worked.

Actually, he was getting quite carried away with it by providing an instantaneous floor show— "Good evening, ladies and gentlemen. Welcome. I hope you are all comfortable on this chilly night. Let's relax together and...." I think that's what he was saying between songs.

I bought my heater and hung around to hear him perform two Enka numbers. His voice wasn't so bad as to cause anyone to say, "I wish he'd wrap up, for godsakes." In fact, apart from a little wobble and an uncertainty at the top of his register, he sounded as good as anything you might hear in, say, the Holiday Inn in mid-America, or on a Saturday night at the local Royal Canadian Legion hall. I liked his performance because it was spontaneous, unpretentious, and honest.

While standing there, I couldn't help but tell myself how karaoke has helped the Japanese express themselves in a way that they will not be nails needing to be hammered down. I've heard unbearably bad renditions delivered with unabashed gusto in karaoke bars, and I know you have, too — performances that have been applauded for courage rather than for artistic merit. But it has mattered not. After all, karaoke is the only entertainment I know of in which there is a kind of nobility for effort, even a nobility for singing atrociously. In that way, after all, you do not expose your friends.

Karaoke can, however, also reveal talent in the mostly unlikely bodies. A few months ago, when I went to Oita to interview the governor of Kyushu, he assigned his six-man entourage to take me to a hostess-cum-karaoke bar. I didn't much like the idea of the tax payers hiring kimono-clad women to giggle at the snap of a finger and top up my whiskey glass while practicing their English; indeed, the musical side of the experience remains memorable.

Halfway through the evening, just as the microphone began to be passed around, I went to the washroom, and, while there, heard an angel singing. Returning to the bar, I was stunned to see the least likely member of the entourage performing like a thrush, his milky-soft voice soaring in "I Left My Heart in San Francisco," which has got to be one of karaoke's most often sung songs.

He was, I recall, a small, somewhat benign individual with ill-fitting false teeth and strands of black hair eked out over his pink head. His eyes shut tightly, his lips caressing every word, he clutched the microphone with a vengeance as he savored his three-and-a-half minutes of absolute, unmitigated glory.

But this was no amateur performance. The voice was not only milky-mellow but even, and the singer's phrasing was impeccable. The only thing that separated this angel from, say, a Tony Bennet or a Perry Como was his diction. "I Reft My Harp in Sam Clam's Disco," he was singing. But that was all right — just as it was in my local electronics shop.

When the man there finished his floor show, and someone at the rear of the shop began to turn out the lights, I told him, best I could, what I thought of his performance. "You sing with great feeling," I said. He must have understood me. Since then, whenever I enter the store he seeks me out, and I suddenly find I am a distinguished customer, indeed, and receive a 10 percent discount on everything I buy.

Thank God for karaoke.

Gift? Or bribe?

March 17, 1990

PEOPLE WHO LIVE in Japan, a friend once told me, have a love-hate relationship with it. One day they adore its carnival spirit, its kindness, and its honesty; the next they ache to go home because the cultural contradictions no longer merely baffle but become unbearably frustrating.

One of these contradictions concerns the matter of key money — those two months of rent that find their way into the landlord's back pocket, never to be returned.

What actually is key money? Why does a self-respecting landlord have the effrontery to ask for it? Where does this expectation come from? I have been trying to find answers to these questions but to little avail because definitions of what key money actually is, and what it is for, vary so drastically from one realtor to the next.

One real estate agent ventured to say that key money was "a sort of deposit to restore the tatami mats after a tenant has moved out of the apartment."

"But what about the two months' deposit the landlord invariably wants in addition to key money? Isn't that to protect against damage?"

"No," said the agent. "It's in case the tenant leaves the place in a dirty state. It will cover the cost of cleaning."

Another real estate agent said that key money was a custom that has been left over from World War II. At the time, the Japanese government allowed landlords to ask for two months' rent as part of the contractual agreement with each tenant. This was done to provide a small cash flow the landlord could tap as and when he wanted to, supposedly to finance property improvements.

"But the war's been over for nearly 50 years," I said. "And in this age, key money is causing a lot of hardship. Too many young people who don't even remember World War II, and who want to rent their first home on limited savings, are suffering badly because of it."

"Yes, I think you're right," the agent said. "But key money is...well, it's a Japanese custom."

The most forthcoming reply to my question was offered by a landlord himself. "Key money is a gift," he said. "It's as simple as that. According to Japanese tradition, you must give the landlord a present."

"It may well be tradition," I said. "But that doesn't make it right. Anyway, why should I give you a gift, and pay the real estate agent you engaged to conduct your business as well? Morally and ethically, none of this is right!"

It sure isn't. I happen to be a landlord myself, owning property in Montreal and Miami. The laws in both places lay down very clearly what a landlord may charge. Rent in advance in the form of a returnable deposit against any damage that may be done to the premises is legal in Florida but not in Montreal. The quickest way to end up in prison in either of these places, however, would be to ask the tenant for a gift of money as a precondition to signing the lease — or make him pay your real estate fees.

The police would call this extortion. They might even term it fraud. Whichever way you look at it, it would certainly be construed as an attempt to obtain money under a false pretense.

Admittedly, Japan and North America are culturally removed from one another, and cultural differences must always be respected. A perplexity, however, exists in the minds of all good, honest people who seek to stay in Japan: Since the country has carved out an industrial revolution to a fair degree by copying the best America has to offer, perhaps the time has come for it to copy the best of those laws the United States has devised to protect its customer.

Asking for key money constitutes fraud. Worse, it takes from the poor and enhances the rich. Isn't it about time the Japanese public rose up with one unanimous voice — to oppose it?

In essence, when an apartment cannot be rented unless key money is paid, it becomes what all too many Japanese real estate agents find too difficult to say because it is far removed from their confrontational nature — a bribe. In any civilized culture, paying a bribe, or asking for one, is considered a loathsome criminal offense. Why not in Japan?

Unfazed by praise?

July 13, 1991

THE IMPETUS FOR this week's column comes from one
written recently by colleague, Mari Shimamura— and
her wonderment, as a Japanese journalist, at the way
Western columnists who write in Western newspapers
and magazines are manhandled by their readers. Here
in Japan, their Japanese counterparts, aren't, of course.
A typical letter to a Japanese magazine about a
columnist's work or opinion, Shimamura points out,
tends to always commend the writer. Letters from
Westerners about Western writers, on the other hand
— even here in Tokyo — "echo with a session of the
Diet, punctuated with the booing of senile socialists."

"Shut up, ya moron!"

"Says who, stupid?"

Mari Shimamura continues, "I've noticed that, as
one of *The Weekly's* accused morons, I'm really only a
modest example. Readers tend to swing indecisively
between calling me 'tasteless' and calling me 'witty.'
Mild stuff compared to the rich abuse heaped upon my
co-columnists, Adrian Waller and David Benjamin.
Whether praised or ravaged, they seem unfazed by it
all, so thick-skinned that they could fall asleep in a
cockroach colony."

Deftly put, Mari. I would, however, take issue on one
point: Are we, your co-columnists, *really* unfazed by
praise and insults? I cannot speak for Benjie. I do

70

remember him telling me, though — shortly after his departure from *Tokyo Journal*, where controversy was his trait — that only when he got nasty letters could he even remotely believe that he was doing his job properly. Letters that commended him sent him to sleep.

Like Benjie, I am both damned and praised. No columnist in his right mind could ever resent a letter that seeks to debate with him, take his opinions to task, or shed new light on what he says. Not at all. What concerns me, though, are those that are designed purely to insult — "Go home, moron."

Yes, I've had a couple of these, too. In fact, shortly before leaving Japan last March, I received an anonymous note saying, "So you're going. Good. Not before time." To *The Weekly's* credit, it does not print anonymous letters, nor those that are insulting — and these are elements that usually go hand in hand, by the way — and commends them to the trash can.

Here, however, hangs a dilemma. What does *The Weekly* do with all those letters, usually angry ones, that criticize a columnist on the one hand while making erroneous statements about him on the other?

These are printed, and rightly so. Readers, after all, are intelligent enough to know when a correspondent is being silly and wrong. The other week, for example, a reader suggested that *The Weekly* get rid of both *Life in Hell* and me. He called my column insufferable and said that the only time I left the foreigners' house where I then lived, was to buy socks. Had he affixed his name to his letter, it might well have been printed because his views are as valid as mine. I would, however, have deserved the chance to publicly respond to him — to remind him of those columns I wrote from Montreal, Singapore, not to mention other large articles from Hong Kong, Malaysia, and from Oita, on Kyushu, in southern Japan.

Another writer maintained the other week that I only ever viewed Japan through rose-tinted spectacles, and his letter was published.

Where was he when I was writing columns about bigotry on Mount Fuji, those obscene comics called *manga*, key money, sexual harassment, and all the baffling paradoxes that make Japan such a difficult but interesting place to be?

Ironically, one of my jobs at *The Weekly* has been to edit — sometimes almost completely rewrite — letters that lambaste me for my views and devalue my work. When I do, I earnestly try to make my critics appear as intelligent, articulate, and forceful as is humanly possible — even when letting them say things about me that I would never tell my worst enemy. Meanwhile, as Mari Shimamura points out, "The editor, a cold-blooded character, seems to encourage the disparagement of his stars, printing an endless stream of hostile letters, and begging for more."

Are Westerners like David Benjamin and me "gluttons for punishment?" Shimamura asks. "Or is something else going on here?"

All I know is that I am trying to perform an honest day's work for an honest day's pay — and have good-natured fun doing it.

Coming and going

December 14, 1991

I WAS BACK AT YOKOHAMA Immigration this week, and, as I waited to be processed, was convinced that if I want to make a lot of money I'm probably in the wrong kind of business. It took all of four minutes for me to renew my work visa, but two hours to buy a multiple re-entry visa which, as you know, is important if I want to make several overseas trips without losing my privilege to work here.

Anyway, while sitting in a coffee shop in Motomachi, I began to think that perhaps my editorial colleague Big Mike and I should enter the very lucrative business of helping people come here, stay, then leave. I see the company now — Millard & Waller, Inc., Comings and Goings.

My idea for this stems from the awful cost of *my* comings and goings — ¥4,000 for a visa, and ¥6,000 for a multiple re-entry permit. That's ¥10,000 already spent and all I've done so far, is stay! But, as we know, there are more expenditures to come — about ¥5,000 to get to Narita Airport, and another ¥2,000 as a kind of admission to the Immigration Lounge, which does not even serve drinks and have soft piano music.

Let me do a quick calculation. My God! I've already spent ¥17,000 and I am still at the bloody airport! And, since I have a wife and a daughter, the visas, the train fare to the airport, and the fee to leave it, or use it —

whatever this ¥2,000 is for — will total ¥51,000. I'm wondering if going is worth it.

"Of course it is — to the Japanese," says a British colleague. "Immigration is huge, huge business."

More certain is that Canada, the United States, Britain, France, and all other European countries, do not charge for visas. Nor do they charge a fee for leaving or returning. Nor is there a charge to enter Immigration. Some countries, how-ever — Hong Kong, for instance — do ask for a small fee for using their major international airport, but, as my colleague adds, "This sum usually takes care of your loose change."

IF, LIKE ME, YOU enjoy music, you will be interested to know about a little record shop I discovered last week-end, in Shibuya. The CDs there cost...wait for it...¥980 for two! That's right. Two for less than ¥1,000 — marvelous old classics, be they pop, jazz, or great performances by some of the world's finest symphony orchestras. For ¥2,000, I bought three recordings by the Berlin Philharmonic playing Liszt, Berlioz, Smetana, Tchaikovsky, as well as a collection of Rossini overtures featuring the London Symphony.

Many of the CDs were displayed on the sidewalk. Inside the shop, at the back, however, I found several cartons that contained the very music I collect. And nearby, there were shelves of fine old jazz recordings — everything from Art Farmer and Dizzie Gillespie to Ella Fitzgerald and Oscar Peterson. Two seasoned Japanese collectors, both of whom said, "I come here to buy the oldies," each held CDs of great bygone opera tenors and Mozart symphonies, and recordings by more recent popular performers like Nat King Cole, Frank Sinatra, and Madonna.

The shop, by the way, is to the right of that curious, pie-shaped police box as you approach it while walking toward Tokyu Hands from Shibuya Station. Let me know what you buy. And don't forget: Not only are CDs a rare bargain in Tokyo, they also make perfectly acceptable Christmas presents.

REMEMBER MY COLUMN, "When mediocrity is beautifully comfortable"? Remember my argument — that Japanese employers tend to hire foreigners who are most like themselves, without talent, without spark, without fire in the belly, so no one around them will ever rock the proverbial boat? Well, my mailbag this week included a letter from a teacher — a Japanese — at Yokohama Gaigo Business Academy who said, "Your opinion is really thought-provoking." He recited the old proverb about the nail that sticks up having to be hammered down, and added that imagination, enthusiasm, or individuality are perceived as a threat to office stability not only in firms, but in schools such as his.

"Strong individualistic views tend to be viewed as outlandish," he lamented. "Individualism is a sort of taboo."

Another reader — a Canadian — who responded to the same column said that all foreigners seeking good jobs here should learn Japanese, and he's right, of course. But he missed the point of my column — that unqualified, unimaginative foreigners who are allowed to do the hiring usually choose people like themselves so they will never feel threatened by having to work with anyone with talent. So the awful problem compounds itself.

Like the Japanese business academy teacher, I feel that this country deserves better.

Students as teachers

July 7, 1990

BENEATH THE LITTLE BUSHES that line Japan's main thoroughfares — and, indeed, in the corners of cabbage patches and gardens that look so appealing from a distance — there are literally tons of beer cans, candy wrappings, old shoes, bicycle parts, piles of mildewed bedding, and whatever else you might want to find there, all waiting to be cleared away. If the Japanese littered in the West like they do in and around Tokyo, they'd barely earn enough money to pay all the fines that would be levied against them by the courts.

Much of the problem is that because they are never supposed to eat in public, the streets have few trash cans. Added to this, too many people eat and drink in their cars and simply throw what they don't want out the window. It's horrible, but it's true. The other part of the problem is that Japan has never taken its environment seriously enough, and, most certainly for granted.

Such wanton neglect, particularly of its beaches and parks, has become so acute an issue among educators in recent years that how *not* to litter — or ecology consciousness — is finally being taught in schools and colleges, before it is too late. At Tokyo Foreign Language College, for instance, teacher Michael Weddington, an American, has formed a multi-faceted club called International Help whose members — a mere 17 students — meet weekly to discuss ways of making their world a better place. One of their first projects was to tidy up their Shinjuku-Gyoemmae campus by gathering scrap paper from the faculty office and carrying it in boxes to a nearby recycling plant.

This weekend, the students are embarking upon something else, and much farther afield — a venture they financed entirely themselves from the proceeds of a campus flea market. Carrying camping equipment and food, they will board the night ferry to Shikinejima, one of the Izu islands about 100 km south of Tokyo. They will also take garden rakes, gloves, shovels, and bio-degradable garbage bags, and, once there, spend two days raking the island clean. "Though relatively unspoiled," says Weddington, "more and more tourists visit Shikine each year, leaving large quantities of rubbish in their wake."

The students will not only pick up what they see, but sort it, putting cans into one bag, bottles into another, paper into a third, and so on. And, between making a little time to relax in an *onsen* and frolic in the sea, they will plant flowers and shrubs to brighten up any public corner they consider drab.

By all accounts, the mayor is looking forward to meeting them. Who can blame him? I'd be happy to encounter *anyone* who volunteered to clean up *my* backyard. "If we pick up lots of cans and want to carry them," says one of the students, Naoko Niizuma, "the mayor says we can even use a truck."

The very idea that there are enough cans out there for this, punches home Japan's environmental apathy. Michael Weddington attributes much of it to the "hierarchal nature of Japanese society," in which — unlike the West — changes are initiated from the top down rather than from the bottom up.

When it comes to important matters, though, Japan can no longer rely entirely on the ingenuity of its leadership. Its politicians aren't known for their love, their passion, or their sensitivity to simple needs, and never have been. That's why Weddington's International Help will also grapple in the coming months with race and cultural relations, human rights, and relations between Japan and developing nations. That's why he is shepherding his students, all but one of them women, to Shikinejima. "I am fortunate," he says, "to have in my club some young Japanese people who definitely go against the national grain."

The students, meanwhile, all of them under 21, are lucky to have a teacher like Michael Weddington. He knows that education is much more than classrooms and textbooks. He knows that it has to be. To teach well is to inspire young people to evolve, and to discover for themselves, all in the ardent hope that they may pass the process on.

So, if those who will rake a little island can make Japan aware that, despite its economic might it has yet to draft even a basic environmental policy, then the lesson — given by the students this time — will have been *very* well taught. Nearly 120 million Japanese, more than half of them living in a 600-km, rubbish-choked strip between Tokyo and Osaka, will have been shown that their country looks better when it is spruced up, and that wanton littering can no longer be tolerated.

Japan in Britain

September 7, 1991

IT WAS AS MUCH a part of Britain as Piccadilly Circus or the Coldstream Guards, and no one ever thought it would fall into foreign hands. But it did — in December 1988. The building that for 130 years had housed the famed clothier, Moss Brothers — it once sold bowler hats and morning coats to prime ministers Harold MacMillan and Harold Wilson, camel hair overcoats to Field Marshal Lord Montgomery, and Harris tweed sports jackets to Bing Crosby and The Beatles — had been bought by the Japanese!

The new owner: the major construction firm, Kumagai Gumi Company of Fukui. The price: $52 million (U.S.) The plan: to turn this, Moss Brothers' birthplace, into a huge complex of offices, stores, and apartments — and provide Kumagai Gumi with European headquarters.

On its last day in the building, on quiet Bedford Street, not far from the Royal Opera House, Covent Garden, Moss Brothers held a farewell banquet, following it with by a brass band parade to its new location a few blocks away. Among the 6,500 guests who were there that day, plenty shed tears of sorrow. But there were also smiles of recognition for a confident future.

Over the past few years, Britons have become increasingly used to the Japanese buying up parts of their country, and, once reticent, they have grown increasingly happier for it, particularly since Japanese companies have built plants that have translated into much-needed jobs. So far, companies like Kumagai Gumi have invested about $32 billion in Britain. That's approximately 60 per cent of the total they plan to lavish upon the 12-nation European Community (EC) when, at the end of next year, it becomes a single economy unto itself, and one the rest of the world must reckon with.

The EC will be a single, marketing area containing some 320 million people — more than two-and-a-half times the size of Japan's population and significantly larger than that of the United States. Economically, if not geographically, Britain will be at the market's very centre. After all, Japan has been investing in Britain since 1972. That's when small but ambitious companies like YKK Fasteners set up in Runcorn, Cheshire, and employed a 100-odd people to turn out zips for trousers, skirts, and luggage. That same year, in peaceful Old Woking, Surrey, Nittan Ltd. began making automatic fire alarm equipment with a staff of only 11 people. Since then, Japanese investment in Britain has exploded, and there are now about 160 Japanese firms there employing some 44,000 people.

In Wales alone, where young boys automatically resigned themselves to one day joining their fathers deep in the coal pits, more than 40 Japanese companies form the heaviest concentration of Japanese investment outside the United States. They include Sumitomo, Hitachi, Toyota, and Sony. In fact, Sony recently announced a $250 million television plant and research center in Bridgend, Mid Glamorgan, and it will create

1,400 new jobs in an area that became more and more depressed as the coal mines began to close in the mid-1960s

Sony already employs 12,000 people in Wales, and that is more than the slimmed-down British Coal, created a decade or so ago to streamline a fading industry and try to save jobs, ever did. By the end of the 1990s, Sony is expected to employ twice that number, and, it says, its investment and interest in Britain will not stop there.

The giant car manufacturer Nissan had plans for Britain, too, and saw them through. In 1984, it opened a $1 billion auto plant in Sunderland, in Britain's economically depressed north-east, and had soon created some 3,000 jobs. This number was later increased to more than 3,500 when one of the company's subsidiaries, Nissan Yamato Engineering, opened a little factory nearby to produce metal stampings. An area, once as foreboding as South Wales, has found new life through Japanese money.

But there hangs a problem, and one that may not be easily solved. It is no secret that Japanese companies have shifted production to countries like Britain to avoid export barriers — huge duties imposed on their products by those countries they enter. It is also no secret that while Japan sees its investments in Britain as a logical place from which to break into the European Community on a vast scale, it is being closely watched by the member countries at large — in the same way as many EC countries have been watching America.

A few weeks ago, for example, an EC committee

ruled that photocopiers assembled by the U.S. subsidiary of Ricoh did not qualify as U.S.-made items and should, therefore, be subject to punitive duties applied to photocopiers that were imported from Japan. But that is not all. An EC regulation that is expected to come into force next month will also require microchip makers to carry out an essential part of the production of semiconductor circuits in EC-based plants — and not just in Britain — if the chips are to be considered EC-made.

By this reckoning, many European industrialists and politicians who would prefer to see Japan scamper from their midst, think that "Made in Japan" labels should, by law, be pasted on all Japanese products that are manufactured abroad. Reason: While Japanese products signify quality to billions of consumers worldwide, they are, for some countries, unwelcome competition — a threat. The EC in particular argues that Japanese companies' overseas production often involves merely assembly — while Japan continues to manufacture the high technology parts at home. In this respect, Sony's decision to build its new research center in Wales followed considerable pressure on Japanese companies by the British government — to upgrade their operations beyond "the screwdriver stage."

"I suppose it's all a question of how you define what is really a home-grown product and what is basically an import," says Tony Moyer, an analyst with SBI Securities (Asia). "There is a feeling that yes, jobs are created and capital is invested, but that the receiving country's technology is not improved, and may be impoverished."

That really is the rub. While Britain — through various projects and incentives — continues to make its green pastures, rolling hills, deep valleys, and historic cities and town attractive to Japanese investment and manufacturing of virtually all kinds, it is viewed by the EC as "the bad boy," And no opponent has been more vocal against it than its nearest neighbor — France.

Most worried about the country-of-origin issue, of course, are the Japanese auto makers. In fact, not since 1957, when the first Toyota Crown cars were loaded onto an American-bound ship in Yokohama have Japan's car makers faced such a daunting future. In those days, Japanese cars rattled, overheated, and were so short of power that they had to be withdrawn from the market. But the manufacturers bounced back.

Today, even during a slump, Japanese cars outperform the market. In the United States, for instance, where car sales fell by 16 percent during the first half of this year, Japanese producers managed to increase their market share. Theirs, after all, were, and still are, the kind of vehicles — compact, well made, and economical — that people wanted, even in Europe.

Of all cars sold in the European Community, a staggering 9.5 percent of them are Japanese. And this may well be part — if not all — of the problems the industry is facing there, despite Britain's insistence on helping such companies as Honda, Nissan, Toyota, and Mitsubishi establish themselves.

"Japan's car makers are suddenly running into a multitude of obstacles in their long drive abroad," says the prestigious English magazine *The Economist.* Adds a Nissan Motors executive, "We are very concerned about the increasing tendency to place a national label on investment."

His company is in a fierce battle with France — where such fine cars as Citroen and Renault are made — over whether the vehicles it makes in Britain are to be labeled Japanese or European, a controversy sparked by France's prime minister, Edith Cresson. She — and her government — have said that 80 percent of the parts of all Japanese cars must be "procured in the EC" if the vehicles are to be considered EC-made and thus be exempt from an unofficial French quota on Japanese imports. And Cresson's words, designed to let the world know that Europe in general, and France in particular, has an auto industry worth protecting, have rekindled a lot of anti-Japanese feelings.

Long known for her harsh judgments and intemperate comments on Japanese trade, investment, productivity, and work ethics, her remarks occasioned the first formal protest from the Japanese government. It also brought out demonstrators from Japan's tiny, but highly visible rightist fringe, to protest against "Mrs. Cresson's Japan bashing" — outside the French embassy in Tokyo.

In London meanwhile, Japanese car makers were warning Britain's trade and industry secretary, Peter Lilley, that unless his government gives them full support in defeating any attempt to limit their exports to mainland Europe, they will curtail their future plans to invest in his country. This has since sparked British fears that EC partners might successfully deter Japanese car factories. The British government, however, says it is determined that EC import laws should not be too restrictive, and has pledged to fight to this end.

"We have always encouraged investment by Japanese companies in the U.K.," says Ken Storey of Britain's Department of Trade and Industry. And concerned that cars produced in Britain should not be counted as Japanese in any system of trade quotas, he added, "All cars made by our industry, whether they are from Japanese-owned companies or not, should be treated as U.K. cars. It is as simple as that!"

Italy — the home of Fiat, Maseratti, and Ferrari — is also reticent about letting a Britain-based Japanese car industry succeed either unchallenged or unmonitored. Recently, it learned about Japanese business prowess the hard way! An Italian chocolate pudding called Tiramisu has suddenly become so popular in Japanese restaurants that young Tokyoites have been ordering two helpings of it, and giving the pasta a miss. The manufacturers were jumping with joy. But not now. Just when they felt that they at last had a home-grown product the Japanese were anxious to buy, they found — to their utter dismay — that a Japanese company had begun to take their business.

Not only had the Japanese slapped a 40 percent tariff on imported Mascarpone, the cheese used to make Tiramisu, but were manufacturing a copy of the pudding itself — at one third of the price!

This, however, is only one of many market complaints being leveled against Japan, and there is none bigger than that which concerns cars. Talks between Japan and EC officials on the problem are continuing, and Britain, alone among EC nations — and a self-confessed beneficiary of Japanese investment — is lobbying hard to ensure that any decision on car imports does not protect European cars at the expense of its own interests. Britain recognizes that in the past few years, its position as a center of manufacturing excellence has been both revived and reinforced by the surge of Japanese investment. And the mutual benefits that this has produced will remain at the centre of Japan's European strategy for many years to come.

These were the conclusions reached at a recent conference in the East Midlands city of Derby — a conference appropriately called "Japan and the Regeneration of British Industry." It attracted top businessmen from both countries as well as a sprinkling of politicians and academics. Derby was chosen to host the conference, by the way, because it is the site of one of the biggest Japanese investments to date: Toyota's $1.2 billion assembly plant with which it hopes to spearhead its post-1992 strategy in an enlarged European Common Market.

Much of the conference concentrated on the Japanese — mostly their car makers — and the impact they have had on British industry, and the impact they are likely to continue to have in the future. One of Britain's leading motor industry experts, Professor Garel Rhys of the University of Wales, told delegates that by the end of the century, the EC will provide a market for some 20 million new cars each year. Of the estimated 2,850,00 that would be made in Britain, he says, the Japanese will produce a million of them — about 500,000 by Nissan, 300,000 by Toyota, and 200,000 by Honda.

To prepare for the future, Rhys says, all the Japanese companies are planning to build engine plants. This, he contends, means that rather than leave their technology at home, they will eventually make Britain a major engine maker capable of producing 2.5 million of them a year by 1995, with Japan contributing only about 600,000. And, as the deputy managing director of Toyota, Takeshi Nagaya, told delegates at the Derby conference, his company's plant would employ 3,000 workers, and that the workforce at large would be motivated, multi-skilled, and multi-functional — all thanks to "continuous training." And, he added, all would-be suppliers would need to demonstrate a matching commitment.

Critics of the Japanese plan for Britain say that Japan is doing exactly what Edith Cresson has said it has done — imposed its work ethic (long hours, short holidays, and undying allegiance to the company) upon other, unsuspecting people. But Britain's powerful trade union movement has already begun to disagree, or, at least recognize, that there has been a trade-off. A decade ago, labor leaders admit, they would not have been nearly so magnanimous in accepting the Japanese way of doing things. Today, though, they have resigned themselves to the reality that the Japanese quest for the market share of almost anything going has swept — and will continue to sweep — across the world.

Virtually all the single union deals with Japanese companies were first engineered — in the 1970s — by Britain's Amalgamated Engineering Union. When it did so, says union president, Bill Jordan, it "broke with a century of tradition, and of accepted rules and restrictive practices." Indeed, he remembers that when the Japanese companies first arrived in Britain — as "manufacturing missionaries, to the oldest manufacturing nation in the world, no less" — there was a lot of indignation. This, however, soon gave way to a practical view of what benefits could be derived from Japanese money. "We as a union," Jordan says, "were deeply worried at the way the quality of workmanship was being undermined in our factories. Companies were cutting quality in order to meet price and delivery demands. So we were very happy to see the Japanese arrive."

More than this, Jordan concedes that Japan has helped rescue huge areas of his country's economy. "Britain's slide into economic decline has resulted in the loss of two million manufacturing jobs, and a severe loss of skills," he says. "Japanese companies have been an island of success in bringing many of these jobs back,"

They have — by being virtually everywhere in the U.K. Of five Japanese companies thriving in Northern Ireland, Takata Corporation makes seat belts and Ryobi Ltd. produces steel-rimmed tires. In Scotland, the Japanese produce about 10 percent of the electronic parts they export. Additionally, Canon assembles photocopiers, and Daiwa Seiko crafts fishing rods in Scotland.

In Scunthorpe, Yorkshire, the road that leads to the bright, new Citizen plant has been named Tanashi Dori. And fittingly, 23 Japanese companies, Hitachi Maxell Ltd. and Toshiba Corporation among them, have established themselves in the new town of Telford,

Shropshire, not far from Ironbridge Gorge, home of Britain's Industrial Revolution. It was there, in 1709, that ironmaster Abraham Darby first smelted iron using coke as fuel. He thus paved the way for the first iron wheels, iron rails, iron steam engine cylinders, cast-iron bridge, iron boat, iron aqueduct, and iron-framed building, as well as the first high-pressure steam locomotive.

In board rooms the length and breadth of the U.K., top industrialists are citing Japanese presence as being largely responsible for "a second industrial revolution' — the reshaping of thinking on how big businesses should be run. Says Sir Brian Corby, "There has been, in some quarters in Britain in the postwar period, an intellectual hostility to industry, coupled with the belief that services are the wave of the future. But, as we have learned from the Japanese, the two sides are complimentary. You cannot deliver economic success without a very strong manufacturing base,"

But that is not all. Corby adds, "We have also realized that if we try,we can be just as successful as the best Japanese companies. We have learned from them lessons that are basically common sense."

What, exactly?

By consensus, British trade unionists and company executives agree that the Japanese have taught them:

- The limitations created by "short-termism"
- Employees must be treated as intelligent human beings, and not automations that can be discarded when they are not longer considered useful
- Small firms as well as large firms are important

- Large companies must treat their key suppliers as partners, even to the point of involving them in the design process

While Britons are basically satisfied, the Japanese are not. At least, not entirely. Japan's ambassador to Britain, Hiroshi Kitamura, says that the 160 or so companies at present doing business in Britain are not nearly enough. "In fact," he adds, "we must work harder to develop the partnership further." But will Britain remain Japan's favorite trading partner in Europe? Or, as some have suggested, would Germany — in view of recently struck German-Japanese car deals — take over?

As long as Britain maintains a firm base of quality suppliers and skilled labor, Kitamura says, it will remain a magnet for Japanese investment for many years to come. More certain is that for the Japanese, the European Community has become the top direct investment target. In a recent report by the Export-Import Bank of Japan — a report based on the predictions of more than 220 Japanese firms that already have a firm foothold abroad — more and more Japanese companies are now planning to establish production facilities or improve existing ones, expand their sales networks, upgrade their service, and buy more and more land for future expansion. It is part of what Tokyo-based economists call "export diversification away from recession-prone America."

When it all becomes a reality, probably within the next four years, Britain will surely be the major beneficiary.

Fear? Or favor?

November 3, 1990

HAVE YOU SEEN THAT rather odd little feature that appears in *The Japan Times* every few days? You know, the one that makes any unsuspecting reader come to believe that *The Japan Times* is really the Prime Minister's public relations department. I am talking, of course, about the *Prime Minister's Diary*. Apparently, this has been running in Japanese newspapers for as long as anyone can remember. Not only have people got so used to seeing it, they no longer laugh at the ludicrousness of it. The Prime Minister, meanwhile, has built up one hell of a PR department — the entire Japanese media, if you ask me.

It *is* ludicrous, isn't it? Or am I going crazy?

8:30 Chairs Cabinet meeting on preservation of the global environment.
9:33 Meets with the Minister for Foreign Affairs.
2:04 Meets with Vietnamese Foreign Minister.
3:31 Meets with Czechoslovakian Foreign Minister.
4:38 Meets with....

Well, the other day, Big Mike and I were sitting in a bar called Jigger when I suggested that if the Prime Minister had to deal with the things we have to deal with each day, he'd end up insane. This is not to detract from his intelligence, of course. It is merely to say that all things being equal, *Adrian Waller's Diary* looks almost as impressive as his:

8:29 Arrives at his desk, befuddled over the odd way he is making a living.

9:03 Meets with Managing Editor to explain, tactfully, that "ALL THE NEWS WITHOUT FEAR OR FAVOR" is a horrible cliché, is trite, and is totally untrue. After all, where is The Leader of the Opposition's Diary?

9:04 Meets with the President of The Japan Times *to say exactly the same thing.*

9:05 Meets with senior newsroom editor to ask why, in God's name, all news stories from the Kyodo News Service say the same things twice.

9:27 Meets with another senior news editor to ask why all captions on photos in Japanese papers tell the reader exactly what they can see for themselves — "Castro strokes his beard," "the Pope waves," "the prime minister sleeps his head off."

9:55 Meets with senior editorial writer to ask why the paper allows people to appear anonymously in Readers in Council. *People like "Name Withheld" and "Angry" have become more and more prolific of late.*

10:00 Meets with Big Mike to discuss The Weekly's *day.*

10:03 Meets with his computer.

After this, I get serious. Today, for example, I edited three stories — two of them very deeply — skipped lunch, laid out two pages, put the final touches to a column, worked out the structure of a big cover story, made six phone calls, argued with Big Mike about a cover photo, edited one of his stories and argued with him about that, almost got into a fight with a junior editor who said that the *Prime Minister's Diary* was fascinating, edited a colleague columnist, faxed David Benjamin proofs of his column, argued with Big Mike about whether it was his turn to buy the beers, then resumed my schedule.

> *5:11 Met with the Managing Editor again about the "Fear or Favor" issue.*
> *5:12 Gave up and bought Big Mike two beers.*

I have to mention the "Fear or Favor" bit because every peeved person who writes to me seems to allude to it. Yet when the slogan was adopted 30 years ago, I was working for my first newspaper — in England. So it isn't my fault.

It's about time, though, that the powers that be changed it. I suggest, "ALL THE NEWS WITH FAVORS AND FEARS," or "ALL THE NEWS WITHOUT FLAIR OR FLAVOR." But, actually, that's really not my idea. It came — naturally — from good old "Angry," bless him, with the support of dear old "Name Withheld," whose hand I would one day like to shake. I think Big Mike would like to meet him, too. That crusty old sunovugun is getting more prolific than ever these days and might like to write for *The Weekly*.

Oh, I forgot to ask the managing editor why the Japanese media always call the LDP the "ruling party." (I learned in my first high school civics class that monarchs rule but that political parties govern.) But that, and other items, are in my Diary for tomorrow: at 10:41.

That's after the prime minister has dropped over to discuss Japan's role in the global environment with me — at 10:40.

Vote Benjie!

August 7, 1991

DID YOU READ WHAT old Benjie had to say the other day about the future of Japan? Did you read his blueprint for *gaijin* rights? Who's Benjie, you're asking? Benjie who?

You know Benjie — David Benjamin, who lives on the opposite page to me in *The Japan Times Weekly*. You don't read Benjie, you say? You prefer me? Well, you *should* read Benjie in *The Weekly*. Sometimes he dredges up ingenious ideas that could well save Japan from economic disaster. His latest is for a new political party comprised entirely of foreigners. He says that I should be a part of it.

"You mean I should *sit* in the Diet," I asked him, "or *go* on a diet?"

"Both, stupid," Benjie said.

I have pondered his proposition carefully, but am rejecting it out of hand. He did not offer me any incentives — like works of art, money, or jobs in case we get elected. At least he could have promised me the Immigration Bureau.

And what about Benjie himself? He only ever suggested this party because, secretly, he sees himself as Japan's next prime minister. Can you imagine it? A man who wears a scraggly gray beard, a Marseille fisherman's hat, and a Hawaiian shirt heading one of the world's richest nations? Is Japan ready for such a figure? Or would he successfully transform it into a Third-World nation virtually overnight?

Can you envision Japan's Prime Minister David Benjamin addressing the Americans on CNN and talking about the "Js" and the "Gs," and allocating special favors to Amalgamated Tanaka, which he incorporated on page three of *The Weekly* a year or so back so his friend Hiroshi could work there and send an unlimited number of faxes to God? How would Benjie react if he discovered that Amalgamated Tanaka had dumped all its shares on the Nikkei just so old Hiroshi, who has paid no income tax for the past eight years, could buy them back at cut-rate prices and start all over again? If that doesn't make sense to you, don't worry about it. Old Benjie would figure it out.

In case you don't know the man behind the photo, I can assure you he is not the Doberman pinscher he may appear to be. There is not an aggressive microchip in his body. At least, not one anyone around here knows about. He sips the occasional beer as if he might not be able to afford the next one, doesn't smoke, no longer says naughty things about women, and saves money by only wearing clean socks on Thursdays. This, of course, would be of obvious help to the National Tax Agency.

He also knows a lot about the Japanese work ethic, too. "All you need do to make your name in a company here," he once told me, "is simply be at your desk — every day. That's all. You don't have to work hard. You don't even have to come up with any bright ideas. Just be there. As long as you're at your desk, every day, on time, you will be perceived as being a loyal and valuable employee."

"Like all the people you hired at Amalgamated Tanaka?" I asked him.

"Yes, exactly! Except that at Amalgamated Tanaka, no one has done any work for some months, which is why Hiroshi keeps faxing God like he does."

"Well, tell me, Benjamin-san. Does all this apply to the 'Gs,' too?"

Actually, he'd call a press conference to answer that one — or even convene a special sitting of the Diet. He recognizes that many "Gs" have about as much status in Japan as itinerant fruit pickers in California, which is why he commissioned Johann Sebastian Bach to write *Air on a G-String* as the party's signature tune. With his fisherman's cap in place, his yellow Hawaiian shirt freshly pressed, his black running shoes brushed, his business bag swelling with comics, Benjie would preside over that press conference singlehandedly — with Big Mike there merely to pour his iced tea.

Once behind the microphone, his gray eyes narrowing, he would espouse all the virtues of foreign labor and how the Japanese know not how to use it. And should this curmudgeon before his time see a reporter not taking notes — or daring to actually *agree* with him — he might raise his voice. Prime Minister Benjie would know exactly what he was talking about, though, because he's been traveling the Yamanote Line for at least two years.

Hey, wait a minute! Stop the presses! Stop, I say! Old Benjie might not be such a bad choice for Japan's next prime minister after all. He would obviously have to disassociate himself with Amalgamated Tanaka, change his running shoes, stop writing his column, and wear a silver tie with his Hawaiian shirt. Those things done, he'll probably do as good a job as anyone.

As Gikon Tamaki says, "At least he's not corrupt."

A pleasant surprise!

February 29, 1992

I WAS IN TABATA the other day to buy, from Sharp
Electronics, the English language instructions on how
to use a complex calculator. Unless I buy another such
item from Sharp, I doubt that I shall ever see Tabata
again. It strikes me, anyway, as a place one only ever
visits when calling upon an aged aunt or a grandmother.

Anyway, while there, I got quite hungry and decided
to look for a Western-style restaurant. But in Tabata,
this corner of old Japan that ambles by contentedly on
the north-eastern curve of the Yamanote Line, there
wasn't much doing. Eventually, however, I came upon
a fine-looking establishment called Good German
Cooking, which was just what I wanted. I am particularly
partial to *Wiener schnitzel*, cabbage soup, and potatoes, and I also like to practice my German now and
then. So in through the big oak door I swept.

When I got inside, I felt a little let down. No one
spoke German at all. In fact, no one even spoke English.
I was in a little Japanese joint, the kind of place I seldom
sample because I find Japanese food distinctly un-
satisfying. Quite frankly, I find the portions in Japanese
restaurants are not much more satisfying than a
Western *hors d'oeuvre*.

The waitress — or was she the owner? — asked me
what I wanted. I, in turn, asked for a menu. Because it
was entirely in Japanese, I couldn't read it. But then, I

saw a notice that advertised that day's "luncheon special" and had ¥680 posted beneath it.

"That," I said, pointing at it. "I'll take that. I like that."

God knows what "that" was. But I thought I'd try it, anyway. When it comes to food, I am very easily satisfied, which is often just as well.

The waitress — a woman of about 60, with gray hair drawn into a bun, and a large maroon cardigan draped over her sloping shoulders — mentioned something about tea or coffee. I nodded at one of them (I couldn't remember which) and she smiled. The ordering part of the ordeal was over.

Actually, it was fairly easy, except, as I say, I didn't really know what I'd ordered. But what else is new? That, in Tokyo, is the story of my life, which, while in the little restaurant, I started to put in order once again. The television was on. The only other customer, a youngish office woman in a blue tunic, was watching a show about fish so intently that you would have thought her life depended on it.

That's not new, either. Every time I turn on Japanese television, someone is either catching a fish, cooking a fish, or eating a fish. The other day, I saw a nature program about fish that eat raw people.

Also in that restaurant, I spotted a large amount of karaoke equipment. At night, it was obviously put to some use. Whoever performed well, though, would hardly get a rousing ovation. The place only seated about 15 people, if that. I think you would get more customers in my Florida bathroom.

Finally the food came and, I have to tell you, it was

more than merely half-decent. Little bits of cucumber stacked in a dish never really sent me wild with delight; the main dish, however, was most appealing. The cook had really extended herself. It consisted of a meat sauce poured over a baked apple. Or was it a pear? It tasted fine, though. And the miso soup was delicious, too, except I had awful problems trying to lift little pieces of tofu out with chopsticks, which I am fairly good at using.

No, I really am! I have become so deft with chopsticks that I can now use them to pick up a pin, though this is the kind of feat I am not called upon to perform very often. Nonetheless, I am very proud of myself for being able to do this.

The soup was so tasty that when I realized I couldn't drink it with chopsticks, I did something for which my mother would have slapped my wrists — hard. I drew the bowl to my lips and, with one or two great slurps, sucked it all my way. I'd say that one of my long sucking-slurping sounds appeared to win some respect in that minuscule joint because the office woman turned to me and smiled. It was a smile that seemed to celebrate my initiation to the Japanese way of doing something important. And, just as I was licking my lips, the waitress deposited a cup of coffee beside me — a full cup, no less! — and I savored that until the woman customer left.

I was alone with the waitress and the cook, after that, and it transpired then that Good German Cooking was a bakery next door, which was closed, and that I had entered the restaurant next to it. Never mind. The price of my meal, by the way, was ¥780. (It seems that the coffee was an extra ¥100, but it was worth it.) And what I had actually eaten was a meat sauce poured over a big slice of daikon, a Japanese radish, which had obviously been cooked in sugar or syrup.

In all, it was an interesting lunch, I'd say, and good value. I'd go to this restaurant again sometime — and I'd take you with me — except I don't think I'd be able to find it. When I left Sharp Electronics, and decided to wander into the side streets, I got lost, which is another story of my life.

For me, Tokyo has become a collage of delightful places and unexpected occurrences that may have slipped away forever.

Japan's board room composer

September 1, 1990

IT WAS A STEAMY summer night at Tokyo's Bunka Kaikan, and a large, dressy audience that included Crown Prince Hironomiya waited eagerly to hear a concert by Poland's Krakow State Philharmonic Orchestra. It was to begin with a symphony by a Japanese composer, and when it did so, strong melodies cascaded through interesting rhythms and fast-changing tempos.

No sooner had the work ended than it was met by thunderous applause, which lasted more than five minutes. Finally, when the ovation could swell no further, the conductor, Roland Bader, pointed to a demure, gray-haired man who was sitting quietly in the audience in a dark suit, and beckoned him onto the big stage to share the adulation. His name: Isamu Kamata, whose *Second Symphony* had now been well and truly played into music history by a world-class orchestra.

"It was one of the greatest moments of my life," Kamata, 62, says as he reflects upon the great orchestral crescendos and the six big bouquets of flowers that were thrust into his arms on that stage by well-wishers.

They were all well-deserved, for Isamu Kamata is no ordinary composer. The president of the computer company, Oki-Unisys, Ltd., he successfully divides his time between being both a creative businessman and one of Japan's most creative musicians. In fact, the

103

sketches for many of his most recent compositions were jotted down during his frenetic schedule of business air travel between Tokyo and London, Los Angeles, New York, and Singapore. "The telephone doesn't ring when you're on an airplane," Kamata says with a smile of satisfaction. "So a good, long flight creates the perfect environment in which I can create tunes in my head and jot them note for note onto paper."

His *Second Symphony* was created like that, between Tokyo and Philadelphia where Unisys, an American company, has its headquarters, and where Kamata used to travel at least once a month. "I had to put this flying time to good use," he says. "What better way is there of doing this than to write a symphony?"

So far, he has produced about 30 musical works, including two big symphonies, a world-famous viola concerto, a piano trio, various pieces for chamber orchestra, and several songs. His list of business posts, meanwhile, finds him with an additional job as managing director of Nihon Unisys Ltd., and memberships of both the Keizai Doyukai, an executives' club, and the Tokyo South Rotary Club, where, until he "got too busy," he was the vice-chairman.

And, for good measure, this imp-like executive officer with dark, darting eyes, who spends about nine hours daily behind his desk in his sparse office on the 10th floor of Mori Building No. 18 in Toranomon, has, for the past 10 years, been the Crown Prince's official piano accompanist. Twice a month, Kamata and the Prince, a good amateur violinist, get together to play sonatas by Bach, Handel, Mozart, and Beethoven, and have a lot of fun doing it.

About his compositions, though, Kamata says, "Music must possess three very important, basic elements — melody, harmony, and rhythm. If any one of these is missing, then it is no longer music at all. It is just a sound." About his business: "Here, the three vital components are quality, cost-competitiveness, and timing. Without each — or all — of these, you are doomed to failure." And, about his double life, he adds, "The moment I enter my office every day, I have to forget my music. Music is complicated. Business is complicated. The two cannot be successfully accomplished together. So, it doesn't matter what wonderful melody I have been listening to on my way to work, or what I am humming as I enter the elevator. When I start work as a company president, the job must have my undivided attention — in the same way that when I am writing a symphony, I must forget that I am the president of Oki-Unisys."

Isamu Kamata was born in 1928 in a small house in Shibuya, the son of a lieutenant general in the Japanese army who saw service during World War II. It was both his father and his mother, in fact, who insisted that their son take piano lessons, to help develop and refine his hearing so he might be able to recognize the enemy aircraft that drew overhead to bomb Tokyo.

Did it? "I don't know about that," Kamata says with a shrug. Much more certain is that out of something so horrible as war — as he often recalls — was born his love for both the piano and for all good music. He was five then, and poised to make music an integral part of his life.

At the age of 13, he started violin lessons, but soon

began to compose little pieces. He penned his first major work in 1946, when he was 18, for the school orchestra at Gakushuu-in, where he was a student. Appropriately called the *Gakushuu-in Suite*, it was given its first performance by the little orchestra in June 1947 under the direction of Kamata's old music teacher, Eiichi Hagiwara.

From his position among the first-violins, the boy was so pleased with what he heard that he was inspired to compose more pieces. One was a little piano trio; the other two were his *First Symphony* and a violin concerto. And he promptly lost the scores of both of them! How? "I lent both to a friend who never returned them," Kamata recalls good-humoredly. Fortunately, however, he was able to piece together all but the third movement of the symphony from the instrumental copies that were produced for the work's first performance in 1948.

Anyone who knows music will quickly detect that these early works were highly influenced by the simplistic romanticism of such composers as the Austrian, Franz Schubert; the German, Felix Mendelssohn; the Frenchman, Georges Bizet; and the Italian, Gaetano Donizetti. "Oh, I agree entirely," Kamata says quickly. "But in those days, you see, I wrote down everything that came into my head."

Later, after studying literature at Keio University, and switching from the violin to the viola, he joined Oki Electric as a salaryman. It was the beginning of his illustrious business career, with music remaining his hobby.

He quickly became manager of the company's business section, then was promoted to group manager, then to director of administration, then to managing director, and finally, to president.

Meanwhile, in the early 1960s, his *Second Symphony* began to take shape. It is a tragic work, indeed, and probably marks the death of his first-born son, Narihiko, who died when he was six from leukemia. "I didn't intend to write sad music," the composer says. "It just came out that way. Normally I am a very happy man, and I think my music reflects this."

Later, as he developed even more as a composer, his music became distinctly *avant-garde*. "It is comfortable and easy to write avant-garde works," he maintains. "But, I think, the best situation is that all people, including the composer, the players, and the audience, can enjoy the music. After playing or listening to it, you should be able to sing it."

By far Isamu Kamata's best work, critics agree, is his *Concerto for Viola and String Orchestra* ("Beauty of Midsummer"), which was completed in 1956, and which has since been performed by the Kobe Chamber Orchestra, the Yomiuri Philharmonic, and America's internationally acclaimed Minnesota Orchestra. Kamata sketched this work during a flight to Seattle, refined it in his room at the city's Four Season's Olympic Hotel, and committed it to paper while seated for hours at a Steinway piano that had been placed in a nearby shopping mall.

Exactly why the piano had been left where it was — probably after a fashion show or a little concert — did not concern Isamu Kamata at all. The fact was that it was there, and he chose to put it to excellent use. "And yes," he reminisces, "shoppers *did* gather round to listen to me as I tried out chords and hurriedly jotted them down, but eventually I became impervious to them."

At home in Yotsuya, where he has two pianos, seven violas, and eight violins, Kamata is working on a third symphony, a group of violin sonatas, and a string quartet that he, the Crown Prince, and two other friends will perform. He was inspired to do this work, he admits, by the Krakow State Philharmonic concert, the more than 20 bouquets of flowers he was given backstage at the Bunka Kaikan — many from such business competitors as NEC and Fujitsu — and the numerous letters he has since received from fans. Without exception, they have urged him to keep on composing.

"I will," Isamu Kamata says. "Wherever I have traveled, music has been a source of constant joy to me. I have a deeply committed feeling that it always will be."

Headhunting in Tokyo

December 21, 1991

A FEW MONTHS AGO, 51-year-old Mitsuo Hirose did
something the Japanese are never supposed to do —
and a dapper, immaculately groomed man named Alex
Tsukada helped him do it. Amiable, self-assured, and
exquisitely talented, Hirose quit his job as the chief
executive officer of a Tokyo printing company, where
his friends and relatives thought he would remain for
his entire working life, and went to work as president
of the medical arm of the giant U.S. pharmaceutical
giant, Johnson & Johnson.

For Tsukada engineering the switch was a coup. Or,
in corporate language, "a high-quality placement that
worked well for the two parties concerned." It was also
all is a day's work for him. A former personnel manager
at both Coca-Cola and Nestlé, Tsukada is a headhunter,
and one of Tokyo's best, who prowls the city by day,
making contacts and keeping his ears tuned to the
corporate world, and making his kill at nights, usually
by telephone from his home.

Mitsuo Hirose was one of his catches.

How times change! Five years ago, a man like Hirose
would never have dreamed of leaving his job, with its
two annual bonuses of three months salary each, and
generous company pension — not to mention the
lifelong friends he studied with and with whom he later
went to work. And he certainly would never have

allowed such a persuasive figure as Tsukada influence his decision. But things aren't what they once were — even in Japan, where the only explanation given for workplace dissent is "that's how it will stay because it is Japanese custom, the Japanese way of doing things." In a perverse way, Tsukada is happy for that workplace dissent.

"Five years ago," he says, his hazel eyes twinkling, "eight out of every 10 Japanese executives I met wouldn't even say hello to me. They hated me. They hated all headhunters. Now they can't wait to ask me how things are going. I tell them they couldn't be better, thank you very much."

Nowadays, Tsukada, who spends two-thirds of his work day bustling around Tokyo to size up his prey, and the remainder in office in Aoyama-itchome poring over resumes and lists of names he has been given of likely candidates who may fill the needs of his firm's clients. These range from the diversified company Procter & Gamble to Bausch and Lomb, which makes contact lenses, and Helen Curtis the cosmetic manufacturer. Tsukada is now able to talk or dine with just about anyone.

And why not? That workplace discontent is growing by the year in Japan, as young university graduates and seasoned executives alike question a work system that keeps them constantly wanting money to spend, yet stunts their progress.

This does not mean that the Japanese businessmen or salarymen have entirely given up the idea of working for one company for life. Not at all. Neither does it mean that headhunters like Tsukada are patrolling the corridors of such companies as Nomura Securities or Sony Electronics snagging executives as they file out for lunch or after-work drinks — bagging trophies, so to speak, for foreign invaders. Nor does it mean that job-hopping has yet reached epidemic proportions in Japan, or that big Japanese companies are flinging open their doors to executives in mid-career.

What it *does* mean, however, is that changing jobs is definitely catching on in Japan as a culturally acceptable thing to do — and quickly.

Last year, for example, nearly 3 million Japanese — about 6 percent of the workforce — switched jobs. Compared with the 13 percent of U.S. workers who change jobs annually, or the 11.7 percent of working Brits who move from one company to another, it isn't much. But it is twice the number it was in 1982, and three times the job-hopping figure for 1972.

This year, 3.4 million people will change jobs and Alex Tsukada, who is both president and a major shareholder of a placement company called Boyden International, will help some of the very best among them do it — "With pleasure," he says. Indeed, due entirely to headhunters like him, the cream of Japan's corporate discontented, including an estimated 90 top executives, will quit their jobs and go where they know their special talents, not to mention their language skills, will not only be respected, but exploited the fullest. They will end up as prizes for foreign companies, particularly foreign banks, which several Japanese already actually run, as well as the Japanese arms of huge Western conglomerates.

According to the Labor Ministry, there are about 370 Japanese already working for foreign companies — men like Tadashi Sakuda, 51, who, until he met Tsukada, thought he was so settled as an executive vice-president at the U.S. headquarters of Suntory, the giant Japanese brewery, that he would remain there to the day he was put out to pasture. It took the determined headhunter one year to convince him he should move to the Japanese subsidiary of Bausch and Lomb as its president, a job he still holds today.

The persuasion wasn't easy, and usually never is. "Sakuda-san moved not because he was going to get a 30 percent pay raise," Tsukada recalls, "but because he would be more autonomous and enjoy a working life free of all the cultural encumbrances." He also recalls how he heard of him through an acquaintance and dropped in to chat with him during frequent visits to Los Angeles."

Back at Boyden International, meanwhile, the triumphant cry went up — "Our Alex has done it again!" But Tsukada himself, who has so far engineered about 400 placements, simply shrugs. "The timing has got to be right," he says. "The people have got to be ripe — half-thinking that something where they are isn't quite what it should be. And that was exactly the case with Hirose-san."

Japan's job-changing trend has spawned numerous companies like Boyden, and they have taken root with abandon. By 1988, 60 such firms had sprung up in the Tokyo area alone. Now, according to Masahide Yoshii, who chronicles them in his monthly *Human Resources Media*, there are more than 400 of them, and all are capitalizing on several changes that began to take place in corporate Japan about 10 years ago.

First, it is no secret that a lot of Japanese are unhappy with their jobs, particularly the time they are expected to spend doing them. Most will stick out their ordeals, and sublimate their sorrows during nightly gripe sessions with similarly disenchanted co-workers over a potent mixture of saké and beer in any one of literally thousands of salarymen's bars, where, in part, Alex Tsukada has been known to ply his trade. But others have different ideas.

When Labor Ministry researchers recently asked 6,000 employees at top corporations how they envisioned their futures, 20 percent said they hoped one day to work elsewhere. Already, the turnover among workers new to the workforce has been estimated at about 15 percent.

Many of these are members of the young, more open-minded army of employees. Appropriately known as *shinjinrui* ("more human race") they are somewhat akin to what the West calls Young Urban Professionals, or "yuppies," and they are placing a greater emphasis on finding happiness and challenge at work, and reducing their office hours so they may spend more time with their families.

In other words, while their elders — even, in some cases, their fathers — chose a company for life and vowed an undying allegiance to it, singing the company song before starting each workday, and resigning themselves to the fact that promotion only generally comes with age and not ability, these new employees don't. For them, there is more to life than working, and they are questioning a system that expects them to stay in one place for so long and wait for their middle-age for promotion.

Lifetime employment took hold in Japan after World War II and is still practiced by about 30 percent of all Japanese companies. In a sense, it is companion to business expansion. When times got tough in steel, ship-building, and textiles, however, several of those same companies actually laid off workers, which is something they don't like to talk about.

Meanwhile, those young men who still pledge allegiance to their employers do so with a subtle difference. "I chose this company," Akiro Okamoto, a research manager at Ricoh Co. admits, "but I didn't choose this job." And he adds, "I love the company, the people, and the benefits, but I'd be more than happy to leave anytime, just to do something more exciting, be closer to promotion, and earn a little more money."

Says another headhunter at Boyden, "There's a seize-the-opportunity mentality among the Japanese now. These guys are starting to think of 'my career' rather than 'my company.' And you can't blame them."

This is where Alex Tsukada comes in. He was born in Osaka, never went anywhere near a university, learned almost-perfect English in a Roman Catholic missionary school in China, where his father was trading, and picked up what he calls "street smarts" while working as a civilian purser on board U.S. naval ships in the 1950s, and on the sidewalks of Tokyo, his favorite city, as he prepared himself for life as a well-rounded executive.

He is good-humored, polite, articulate, and shrewd beyond words. And he cashes in, happily, on all of the elements that present themselves in the Japanese workplace — not only of dissatisfaction and disappointment, but of uncertainty, too.

"First of all," he says, "I never just phone someone 'cold.' If I'm interested in talking to him, I'll spend a lot of time arranging a proper, formal introduction through a former workmate, even a relative." That done, he then tries to arrange a meeting over a drink or two in a local cocktail lounge. "Just as busy men don't like being phoned in the office," he adds, "so they prefer to discuss their jobs outside, during informal, clandestine meetings in places where they aren't likely to be seen or overheard."

From then on, the questions that flow depend on the type of executive being wooed. More certain is that rather than put direct questions to his prey, Tsukada the amateur psychologist is more likely to "fish," to find out the area's of the executive's discontent, then work on them, subtly — "Are you happy with what you're doing? Do you think you have enough opportunities for advancement? Do you think, maybe, that there's a better position for you elsewhere? If so, what would you expect from it?"

It is a skill that may well come naturally to Alex Tsukada, and one that combines intuition, knowledge of the corporate workforce, and plain common sense. Just as he predicted — in 1976, while at Nestlé, and four years before he joined Boyden — that the ailing Japanese textile industry would soon dump a pile of brilliant young executives into the employment market place who just had to be snapped up, so he knows that about 180,000 similar people are working in the United States alone, with many thousands more stationed in those corners of the globe in which Japan has consolidated strong markets. These workers, he says, not only learn the local language, as well as English, but develop a more mobile, autonomous way of life both at home and at the office. In so doing, when they return to Japan, as most of them invariably do, they bring solid, specialized experience, a knowledge of the world, and, having tasted better times, a keen desire not to work for a Japanese company in Japan.

Put differently, Japanese executives like Mitsuo Hirose, who have had schooling or major assignments overseas, are prime targets for international companies that have set up back in their homeland, and are, therefore, the best candidates for top jobs — and excellent candidates for an eager Alex Tsukada, too.

Although some large Japanese companies have begun to move away from the idea of offering lifetime employment, however, they have yet to fling open their doors to executives in mid-career, even those with international experience, which is also where Alex Tsukada steps in.

Ask him, and other headhunters, about such employees as Yasutaka Izumura. Like Mitsuo Hirose, he seems to typify those executives who switch careers because theirs was a typical dilemma. In 1979, Izumura graduated from the University of Tokyo's prestigious law school and joined Daiwa Securities, Japan's second largest brokerage firm. "But I was only ever one of the crowd there," he says — even after the company sent him to the Wharton School of the University of Pennsylvania in 1983 to get a master's degree in business administration.

On his return, he was further disappointed that Daiwa did not utilize his newly acquired skills. Worse, he suspected that his absence from the firm had taken him out of line for advancement. So, in 1987, he took a bold step. With a headhunter's help he quit Daiwa to become an analyst at the Tokyo branch of the brokerage firm, Smith Barney. Two years later, and with his sights set even higher, he became the senior analyst at Goldman Sachs, the prestigious investment house.

Understandably, those Japanese workers already with foreign companies in Japan are eagerly sought by new foreign companies that are arriving from abroad. They are, of course, *perfect* candidates for Tsukada, and he fervently seeks them out, too.

Added to this — and whisper it, please, for it has long been a cultural no-no — Japanese companies are starting to steal top people from their competitors, particularly those who are bilingual and have broad experience!

One Japanese firm told Tsukada to keep its efforts to lure a senior research and development engineer from a rival organization a carefully guarded secret. The management was not only worried about "public embarrassment," but "saving face."

To alleviate the problems, Tsukada arranged for the man to accept a job in a "dummy" *foreign* firm to disguise the fact that he was being "stolen" by a Japanese company — and to make the big, final move six months or so later. The plan worked superbly, as it usually does.

"I do this sort of thing quite often," Tsukada says, with another shrug. But then he, like other top headhunters, considers himself more of a management consultant who does a lot of counseling and hand-holding, and gives free advice to both executives and companies alike.

One thing Tsukada never fails to tell his clients is, "Look on your own front doorstep. There are literally hundreds of Westernized Japanese managers working in such places as New York, Los Angeles, and London, and those who are homesick nearly always respond to the right overture that will promise them a good job back home."

Enter yet another factor: Because of the recent rise in the yen against most major world currencies, many long established Japanese firms are restructuring. In just 12 months, 400,000 jobs have been lost as work has shifted offshore. Thus, a lot of good people are looking.

Conversely, Tsukada is quick to point out that many foreign firms stumble badly when hiring Asian nationals — by over-emphasizing fluency in English. Reasonable linguistic proficiency is, of course, important, he says, but extreme fluency may often mask certain deficiencies. Or, to put it his way: "The guy who speaks perfect English may be lacking in other smarts."

A recent trend, Tsukada knows, is to install top Japanese executives in foreign companies' Japan subsidiaries — for a variety of reasons. Companies like IBM, Kellogg's, McDonald's, Mobil Oil, and the chemical company W.R. Grace, all know that even those foreigners who eventually master the Japanese language cannot ever hope to match a native speaker for the contacts he can build.

Japanese usually make lifelong friendships during their school years; for graduates of elite universities, these friends form an invaluable network that runs through government and business, and is often a passport into Japan's complex distribution network. Besides this, the high cost of keeping expatriate executives in Tokyo is exorbitant. Western-style housing in downtown Tokyo can cost as much as $10,000 U.S. a month. So offering generous pay to a competent Japanese is not only more practical, but can, in the long run, prove to be more economical, too.

Foreign firms do not generally offer lifetime employment, but they can give an ardent Japanese a spot on an international team, and for some, this alone justifies the risk of quitting a Japanese company. Additionally, Western firms also generally offer more money, greater responsibilities, and chances of a much faster promotion — without all the cultural baggage.

Working for foreigners can sometimes have a glamorous side, too. After spending 20 years promoting British exports to Japan, Kazuichi Kocho was aptly rewarded by being installed as a Member of the British Empire, an honor he proudly displays on his *meishi!* "The most important variable was the job itself," he says of leaving a Japanese company to work for a Western one. "Now I can exercise discretion and responsibility."

In the years ahead, as more and more open-minded young people enter the Japanese workforce with thoughts like these, the country's lifetime employment practice will probably disappear. Japanese employees will still be loyal, says Boyden's general manager, Stanley Holt, "but it won't be a blind loyalty anymore."

Meanwhile, Alex Tsukada plans to spend as much time as he can doing what he does best, except that his competition promises to be greater. By the end of next year, he estimates, Tokyo will have about 500 headhunting firms, and these will eventually level off at around 600. Many of them won't be as large as Boyden, or as successful or dynamic. But they will be there, nonetheless, to supply a need.

"The Japanese work ethic," Tsukada says, buttoning his gray suit jacket, "is changing."

His hunch now is that there will a lot more men like Mitsuo Hirose, just waiting to be bagged.

Reading between the lines

March 21, 1992

I RECEIVED THREE LETTERS the other week, the first from a man named Takeshi, who has never been out of Japan, the second from a 29-year-old Brazilian named Moniika Vega, who has recently ridden herself into *The Guinness Book of World Records* by becoming the first woman to circumnavigate the world on a motorcycle, and the third from a former colleague professor at the University of Montreal, who spent many years traveling between Canada and the United States to write books on crime and women's issues, all of them properly published.

Takeshi says, "I read your column each week with interest but suspect, reading between the lines, that there are things about my country that frustrate you." Moniika, meanwhile, remembers how I profiled her in *The Weekly* and, in a small way, helped her get Japanese sponsors so she could chalk up kilometers in Japan by riding from Tokyo to Fukuoka and back. She asks, "Do you remember me?"

Of course I do. She told me how she had to fight every inch of the way to get her project off the ground, and that once it was, she needed to penetrate all manner of cultural barriers to keep it going. In Libya, for instance, she was stopped by the police at every major junction. "They had not often seen a blonde riding a motorcycle," she reflects. She was refused admission to other Muslim countries, however, because women there are not allowed to drive at all.

My professor friend, meanwhile, who knows I am in Japan purely to enjoy it, asks, "What in God's name are you doing working for a Japanese newspaper? Don't they try to censor what you write so that you can only present a positive picture of their country to the world? I am told that no one outside Japan takes a lot of those Japanese papers very seriously anyway, because they omit important news and run all kinds of articles on their editorial pages that are, when it comes right down to it, pure fluff, propaganda."

Yes, Takeshi. There are things about Japan that frustrate me, and my answer to your question might also address the professor's. No one has tried to censor me in Japan, nor expect me to write propaganda. And if anyone ever did, I would catch the next plane out of Narita Airport. Censorship is something I will not tolerate. There are, however, some Japanese people in moderately high places who would like to cut out my tongue. They have been raised to see only the good in their country and their institutions and wish I had never criticized either of them, even though I have only ever done it with affection.

What I have said about the Japanese way of doing things — the dishonesty of key money, for instance, the bonus system being "social engineering," and how young, talented people are being manipulated by older, spiritually impoverished souls who could never aspire to achieve what they have achieved — has drawn the ire of...guess whom? You're right — the spiritually impoverished!

Nonetheless, last November, when a Japanese publisher asked to see a collection of my columns for possible publication as a book, I braced myself for instant rejection. I was quite prepared to hear that my work was "too strong," "too critical," "too controversial," too anything else that might be going. To the publisher's credit, however — and this has helped reinstate some faith in Japan's print media — the columns were deemed totally acceptable, with no questions asked.

The other night, in fact, the editors told me that despite what other Japanese people thought, whomever they were, and wherever they worked — and some of them, by the way, will tell you they are journalists — those columns I submitted for publication were highly appreciated because they did not represent an automatic, unequivocal approval of Japan. They truly were a foreigner's view, and one that deserved to be taken seriously, purely for what it was.

This gave me some heart because — please read between the lines, Takeshi — there have been times when I have wondered if a columnist in the Western sense of the word, and in the Western tradition, would really have a place in Japan — even though Japan has been trying so hard to become a part of the world at large. Do you see a shocking irony? So do I. Anyway, my book, *Being Here, A Western journalist's view of Japan*, will be published in only days now.

You may now be asking how a Brazilian woman who chose to borrow a friend's Honda motorcycle so she could ride into *The Guinness Book of World Records* figures in all of this. Well, it's really quite simple. "If you are really committed to circumnavigating the world, and you feel it must be done," says Moniika Vega, "you have to find a way of circumnavigating the ideas and attitudes of myopic people. It's the only way."

I know that both Takeshi and my professor friend would agree with that. You probably do, too.

- *Editor's note*: Being Here, A Western journalist's view of Japan *was published by Yohan Publications Inc. in April 1992.*

Appreciatively yours

November 16, 1991

IN A FRENZY OF compulsive enthusiasm the other day, a wealthy, German pearl trader named Rudolf Voll wrote three letters to as many Tokyo newspapers. The first denounced people who waste food at buffet luncheons. The second called JR's "no smoking" signs hopelessly inadequate. The third suggested new ways of disposing of the dead.

"Why stuff corpses into the ground we don't have enough of?" wrote Voll. "I've told my wife to take my body and throw it into the ocean. Don't burn it. Think of the pollution it will create. Don't bury it, because that creates unnecessary manpower. Give my body to the fish. It's only fair. I've eaten enough of them in my time, now they can eat me."

Eighty-one-year-old Rudolf Voll has been bombarding newspapers with letters like this for as long as he can remember. He has written more than 6,000 of them in all, and mailed them to 256 different publications ranging from *Newsweek* and *The New York Times*, to *The Nippon View* and the *Tokyo Weekender*. So regularly have his comments appeared in Letters to the Editor columns, from Singapore and Bangkok to Hong Kong and Tokyo, in fact, that readers constantly ask who he is.

"Would the real Mr. Voll please identify himself?" one demanded after seeing his letters in *The Straits Times*. "Maybe he doesn't even exist."

125

He does, indeed, and when prominent German politicians come to Tokyo and ask to meet him, he unmasks himself willingly. Other times — and because there is too much traffic rumbling past his house, on busy Highway No. 1 in Hakone, creating too much noise for him to either sleep or concentrate — he shuts himself away in his daughter's Tokyo condominium, or the little hole-in-the-wall trading post near the overhead railway lines in Yurakucho, where he sells his pearls and types his letters on a little portable typewriter.

Voll does not profess to write pearls of literature, though. In fact, his letters are usually verbose and ragged. Rarely, however, do they cease to be provocative. When a *Hong Kong Standard* reader suggested that he only ever wrote to newspapers because he aspired one day to run for public office, Voll dashed off a letter, which was also printed, thanking the man for mentioning his name!

Intrigue pursues him. "He's the most interesting person I've ever read," Jo Ann Onusa of Yokosuka wrote in the *Asahi Evening News*. Another reader, Rick Nelson of Matsuyama, said, "Voll should be given his own column so people like us can avoid his letters. I am tired of them, due to their vacuous content and sheer volume."

Voll shrugs. "People want to make me disappear," he says. "I couldn't care less."

Not only do they love to hate him, they also love to insult him. He somehow actually thrives on being labeled everything from "a dreary old bigot" and "a fascist pig," to "a silly old crank" and "a regular pain in the ass." He has been called "Rude Voll" and "Vile

Rude," but both names have left him monumentally unfazed. "Half of my enemies can't even spell my name," he says.

Some readers have argued with him in print for many years. "One such crazy man," Voll remembers, his craggy face crinkling into a grin, "was obviously a Bolshevik who was paid by Moscow to use the press to attack me. He called me a Nazi and objected to my beady eyes." One day, Voll suggested that he meet his opponent for a quiet dinner, and got an Indian journalist friend to arrange it at the Tokyo Foreign Correspondents' Club. Thereafter, the two men became friends, though they continued to lambaste each other with words as if nothing had happened.

Those who know Rudolf Voll well see him as he really is: a lovable, silver-bearded old eccentric with twinkling eyes and a fine head of hair — a cross between a carved doll from the Black Forest and a biblical prophet — who writes without fear or malice, and with the freshness of a wayward child and the demeanour of a naughty boy wanting to change the world.

Once, he would have liked to have done so. He was born in Berlin in 1911, the son of an impoverished tailor who lacked even the money to send his only son to high school. Young Rudolf had different ideas, though. He was only 11 when he wrote his first important letter — to the Berlin School Board, asking if it would let a poor boy become a student without a fee. The board agreed, and Voll remembers today, "From then on I learned the power and the permanence of the written word."

In college, he studied auto design and learned English. When he sailed to London to practice it, he found that no one understood him. Soon, he developed his passion for writing letters, never for a moment thinking it would make him a celebrity halfway across Asia. In 1929, he began writing to such newspapers as *Die Morgenpost* and *Berliner Zeitung*, mostly about cyclists' rights, the need to protect nature, and smoking. ("I started smoking cigars when I was five and stopped when I was 15," he recalls.)

Since then, he has become phobic about tobacco smoke. When he attends Tokyo's monthly pearl auction, he wears a mask — "because of all the inconsiderate people who go there, too. It makes me so mad!" At the next auction, he threatens to wear a mask and a diver's goggles, and carry a cylinder of oxygen on his back.

"And look at this!" he screams, pointing to a photograph of a pillar at Narita Airport. "That's what I call the 'sayonara' pillar because it's the last pillar anyone sees after leaving Immigration. Look at it! Why is it so shabby? It needs painting!" And he adds, "This is not my pillar. I get nothing out of writing about it. I'm simply showing my pride for the place of my abode."

Rudolf Voll came to Tokyo in 1937 as a political refugee from Nazi Germany, and found life harder than he thought it ever would be. Originally, he wanted to design cars, except that on his arrival, Japan only produced military vehicles, and the military wouldn't trust a German. So he turned to pearls. When the postwar occupation forces forbade pearl trading, he took up furs, audaciously making the military his biggest customer. One day in 1946, the military accused Voll of doing something else that was prohibited in those postwar years — dealing in gold. It later conceded it was wrong, however, and, to make amends, found him an apartment in which he could continue to trade in furs unimpeded. Voll later returned to pearls, establishing his company, Pacific Pearls Inc., and swiftly became known not only as a world authority on Japan-cultivated pearls, but as a Tokyo eccentric as well. He thought nothing, for instance, of appearing in a fez, a fedora, even a burnoose! Sometimes he wore plus fours and flowing black capes.

His greatest letter-writing triumph came in 1947 while living, for two years, in New York City. He was so appalled at the way the police treated local drunks who assembled near his room in a boarding house opposite a gymnasium in Manhattan's German district, that he wrote to *The New York Times* about it. His letter was printed, and this inspired him to write more.

In Tokyo, meanwhile, he had been conspicuous by his absence, though it was not long before his presence was to be felt once more. In 1953, *The Nippon Times* wrote an editorial about his mink bow ties, his mink vest, and his mink Tyrolian hat! Rudolf Voll acknowledged this the best way he knew — with a letter.

Nearly 40 years later, he is still finding words to express his views on almost everything, and with panache. He rises daily at 3:30 a.m., and begins to scratch the notes that will become that day's letters. He seeks to write three a day and has been known to produce as many as eight! Then he mails them and waits. Not long ago, four different Tokyo newspapers published four different Voll letters on the same day.

Every month, Voll travels to Hong Kong on business,

and he and his wife Frieda visit their daughter Aloha in Bangkok, or their son Fuji in America. Rudolf Voll confesses to writing most of his letters on airplanes.

Back in Japan, he remains an unforgettable sight. He wears a brown beret and a long, blue coat, and wields an umbrella a wealthy girlfriend gave him back in 1939. "I used to have a brown coat," he laments, "but I left it on an airplane and it ended up in the garbage."

His success is simply explained: "Wherever I go, I write a letter. But I never raise a problem without suggesting a solution." And remembering how he grew his beard two years ago because he thought he looked too young — at a time, he feels, when the elderly do not garner the respect they deserve — he adds, "Don't let people shove you around, and don't, for God's sake, think of retiring."

He certainly doesn't. He has too many letters to write for that.

Morning ritual
December 8, 1990

SOME WHILE AGO, A READER compared me with syndicated columnist Mike Royko, which was a compliment indeed. I happen to think that Royko, who writes for *The Chicago Tribune,* is the one of the best columnists around. He infuses what he thinks, sees, or hears into a piece of writing so laden with ironies and poignant truths that, if it doesn't make you laugh, it will surely make you cry.

For me, it does both. So each day, when I pick up *The Japan Times,* Royko's crisp words are the first things I look for, and when he isn't there, as he often isn't, I immediately switch to the sports pages to see how badly my hockey team, the Montreal Canadiens, has been doing. Thus begins my morning ritual.

One woman I know does the crossword puzzle long before she even reads the front page of her newspaper. And my colleague, Big Mike, who is becoming more and more obsessed with the huge flow of trade that flows between Japan and the United States, turns straight to the financial page to see how the dollar is faring against the yen. If the dollar is up, his language turns the air blue. If it is down, he chuckles and muses, "Hey, Goat! You and I just got a pay raise!" He says that every other day because, as you know, the dollar has been bouncing up and down of late.

If the San Francisco 49ers have won another game

in America's National Football League, Big Mike tells the entire staff — even people like Yoko, Manako, Kasuko, and Taka, who couldn't care less because they've never even heard of the 49ers — that his favorite team is "kicking butt." And they probably don't even know what "butt" is.

I don't know what Mike reads next in *The Japan Times*. All I know is that I also look to see how the dollar is doing, then read the National Business Briefs before turning back to the sports pages for the Sports Briefs. I want to know what fighter in some far off land has been beaten into a coma, what Bulgarian weight lifter has been done for steroids, and what sumo wrestler has grown so fat he can no longer walk.

I then read the front page, except I've usually seen this long before it's even printed — while it is being pasted up in the composing room. Somewhere along the way, I also glance through the World News Briefs to see how my country — Canada — is doing.

"Who cares about Canada?" says Big Mike. "It could be blown off the map and you wouldn't even miss it. Anyway, the 49-ers are *really* kicking butt!"

What he forgets is that I have two countries, so I also want to know if Arsenal thrashed Liverpool in English League soccer, and who won the Daily Mail Brass Band Competition at the Royal Albert Hall.

Since only one cartoonist in the entire world has ever made me laugh — Giles, who worked on one of my first newspapers, the London *Daily Express* — I skip the funnies. Humor so often fails to cross ethnic borders, anyway, so it's usually a waste of time when it comes to newspaper cartoons. Besides, on some days, nothing will make me laugh. If I want another chuckle, I quite often turn back to crusty, cynical old Royko to see if he said anything I missed the first time I read him, and there usually is. Oh, yes. Then I finally read the front page to make sure it hasn't changed since I last saw it. Often there's quite a chuckle there, in the headlines.

Then come the Classifieds. The job section: *Help Wanted — Male & Female.* "Female impersonator wanted for nightclub act." You know the kind of stuff.

Why the Classifieds? Well, back at the *Daily Express*, a story goes that the publisher, Lord Beaverbrook, once collared a young reporter in the elevator and asked him, "Are you happy working here?"

"Oh, yes Sir," the reporter replied.

"Well, you're fired!" Beaverbrook is said to have snapped back. "Happiness at work makes for terrible lethargy."

I've never forgotten that. That's why I'm always looking for another job.

Here's one:

Juggler, rapper, stilts, magicians, mimes, other performers and campaign women with proper visa.

Last week, a bar in Shinjuku was looking for a bouncer. That was in *Help Wanted — Female.* The best job suggestion, however, came the other day from another reader. "Tell dear old Adrian," he wrote to Big Mike, "that when Royko retires he can move to Chicago!"

After the Classifieds, I have another coffee and read the obituaries. If my name isn't there, I get dressed and dawdle off to work thinking that it's about time old Royko *did* pack it all in — just to give someone else a chance. If he did, he'd be bowing out at the absolute peak of his prime, while his brain is still functioning because no one has yet punched him out.

He should have no worries about being written into posterity, by the way. Clever guys like him who see this crazy world as it *really* is — and who are part of many a morning ritual — are remembered for a long time.

Hiroshima remembered
August 17, 1991

I WAS NINE WHEN THE atomic bomb exploded above
Hiroshima at 8 : 15 a.m. on August 6, 1945. Akihiro
Takahashi was just approaching his 14th birthday. I
first heard about the attack when my mother ran into
the garden of our house in Kent, England, crying,
"Something terrible has happened to the Japanese!"
Akihiro Takahashi knew about it because when the explosion occurred, he and 60 schoolmates were sitting on
benches in the yard at Hiroshima Junior Middle School
No. 1, waiting to greet their teachers. A few minutes
earlier, he and one of his friends, had actually spotted
the U.S. Air Force B-29 (nickname: "Enola Gay") from
which the bomb was dropped, but they had no time
to share their reactions to it. In the second or two it took
them to realize exactly what it was they were seeing
against the clear, blue sky, the world stopped.

"At least," says Takahashi, "that's the way it seemed."

First, darkness descended. Then the explosion, 580
meters above the city center, was followed by an im-
plosion that was so intense that it sucked out Takahashi's
breath, and his fingernails. The blinding white heat,
meanwhile, which for a fraction of a second reached
between 3,000 and 4,000 degrees Celsius, seared off his
ears and turned his flesh to liquid.

"What would you expect?" he recalls. "My school
was only 1.4 kilometers from the hypocenter."

Had he been a kilometer closer, he would have been reduced to ashes or melted like the iron girders, the tiles on roofs, and the stones that lined the banks of the city's seven rivers.

So vast was the devastation that killed an estimated 140,000 people, half of them instantly, that it inspired in me a dream. One day, I told myself, I would see Hiroshima first hand. I would hear what happened from the survivors themselves and learn how they have resiliently rebuilt both their razed city and their shattered lives.

Akihiro Takahashi had a dream, too. By showing his wounds, sharing his memories, and using his own words to relive them, he would tell us all how war is most cruel to those who never wanted it. Last week, he and I met — in Hiroshima. We shook hands and swapped stories.

"I'm so glad you came to see me," he said in a firm but soft voice. "Through writers like you I can let the world know what really happened to the people of my city, and I can do it in the sincere and ardent hope that a tragedy like this will not be allowed to occur again."

Takahashi and I came together in what seems to have been a most suitable place — at an exhibition titled "War and Peace," one of many anti-war events that have been organized world-wide since 1982 by an organization called Soka Gakkai International. The group's first exhibition, "Nuclear Arms: Threat to Our World," was held at the United Nations Headquarters in New York City during a special session on disarmament. It was seen by more than 1.2 million people in 16 countries, including Canada, West Germany, France, Greece, China, and the Soviet Union, and also traveled to every major city in Japan. Indeed, so great was its impact that it was expanded to form "War and Peace," which made its debut at the U.N. in 1989.

At its opening in Hiroshima last week, about 300 guests, including three peace activists from the Soviet Union, gathered to hear a slew of speeches and view some of the most powerful news photography the world has ever known — pictures that speak more than a million words about a century of war, and the hope for a century of lasting peace. One of the most poignant talks was delivered at a reception later. As the guests — most of them men who provided a sea of blue suits and red and white rosettes — sipped beer and munched on tempura, the United Nation's representative in Tokyo, an elegant Pakistani named Mian Qadrud-din, said, "There is no better venue for an exhibition on war and peace than the City of Hiroshima. It reminds us of the horrors of modern warfare."

Takahashi hung onto the speaker's every word. When Mian Qadrud-din continued, he began to nod.

"Hiroshima's reconstruction today," the U.N. man said, "demonstrates to us the indomitable will of mankind to struggle by peaceful means to build a prosperous society...the exhibition we saw this morning is, indeed, very effective in achieving public understanding of peace."

Akihiro Takahashi has always had a deep respect for the efforts of Soka Gakkai International, too. He likes the way that, completely independent of government, it confronts global issues and organizes exhibitions to raise the public consciousness of them. In fact, he has attended previous similar shows — "Nuclear Arms:

Threat to Our World," for example, when it went to Geneva — and made sure he was always around to explain the horrors of Hiroshima to such people as the Pope and Mother Teresa when they visited the city's Peace Memorial Museum.

Soka Gakkai was founded in 1930 by author and educator, Tsunesaburo Makiguchi — to promote the practice of a form of Buddhism espoused by a monk named Nichiren Daishonin, who was born in 1222 and who died in 1282. It was left to one of Daishonin's disciples, however, Nichiren Shoshu, to spread the word. Central to Daishonin's teachings was respect for "the innate sanctity of life." But he also believed, invincibly, that a fundamental change in the life of one person could bring about the reformation of society as a whole. Those who were first to understand this were intellectuals. Thus, the organization, originally called Soka Kyoiku Gakkai, (Educators Society for the Promotion of Values), drew its early membership primarily from teachers and professors.

Under Tsunesaburo Makiguchi's leadership, the organization fought to uphold freedom of religion. One of its first crusades, then, was to resist the efforts of the Japanese militarist government when it tried to enforce State Shintoism as a means of rallying the spiritual resources of the Japanese people behind its war effort.

Soka Kyoiku Gakkai ran into difficulty, though. For one, its voice was not heard by enough people during those pre-World War II years. In fact, by 1942, it had only 3,000 members. For two, in July, 1943, it leaders, including Makiguchi and the general director, Josei Toda, were imprisoned as "thought criminals." Despite being brutally tortured and deprived of food, Makiguchi, who was already 72 at the time of his arrest, refused to recant or compromise his convictions. He died on November 18, 1944, in the Tokyo Detention House — today the site of Ikebukuro's Sunshine Hotel — of malnutrition. Josei Toda, meanwhile, survived his ordeal and was released from prison on July 3, 1945, just weeks before Hiroshima was bombed and Japan surrendered.

Although ill and emaciated, he immediately set about the task of rebuilding the organization, which had all but disintegrated under the pressures of wartime persecutions. In 1951, when Toda became the group's second president, he renamed it Soka Gakkai (Society for the Creation of Values). The change made his point that such important activities should no longer be confined to educators, but opened to all people, in all spheres of life. By the time of his death in 1958, he had seen the membership grow from 3,000 teachers and scholars, to the men, women, and children of more than 750,000 Japanese households.

In 1975, Soka Gakkai was registered as a non-governmental, international organization, and, by the early 1980s, was working with, or being sponsored by, various United Nations agencies and committees. Thanks largely to that link — and a flood of exhibitions and seminars it has organized on topics like children's art, the environment, and Third-World poverty — it now claims 8 million Japanese households. Additionally, it has another 1.3 million members in 115 countries on six continents and keeps them informed with its own newspaper, 35 magazines, and various newsletters, a total of 10 million of which are published each year.

Also in the years since its founders were persecuted, Soka Gakkai has broadened it horizons — to focus world attention on poverty, the environment, racism, human rights, and all manner of other discrimination similar to that remembered by another Hiroshima survivor I spoke to, a resilient, bird-like woman of 60 named Etsuko Kanemitsu. She remembered how hard it was, having spent much of her teens recovering from intense burns, to find work. "Too many people thought that all those who lived through the explosion were in some way permanently contaminated with nuclear radiation," she says. "Most firms refused to employ us because they thought we would be weak people, constantly asking for time off. Some were sure we would create other problems for them — by dying on the job."

Kanemitsu never did find a job. "I eventually gave up," she told me. But she did it philosophically, re-markably so. "My mother suggested that I stay at home and sew kimono," she recalls. "That way, I'd at least be skilled at something."

"War and Peace" was also attended by peace activists, ecologists, politicians, nuclear physicians, from as far afield as the United States and the Soviet Union. Together, members and their guests viewed photographs of the battlefields of World War I and World War II, the soup queues of the Great Depression, the bloodshed in Vietnam, the famine and starvation in Sudan, the 1986 nuclear in-cident at Chernobyl, and, of course, the death and destruction in Hiroshima. Among the exhibits was a photograph of Akihiro Takahashi's deformed right hand, and, in a small glass case, one of his claw-like fingernails.

Grotesque? Of course. But then so was Hiroshima's inferno, caused mainly by thermal radiation — just as school was about to start on that August morning.

At the first flash of light, Takahashi, temporarily blinded, fell unconscious and estimates he did not come to for about 10 minutes. When he did, he recalls, he had been thrown about 15 meters. His school had been reduced to rubble, the air was full of black smoke, and the place where he lay was strewn with the charred and broken bodies of his school friends. The remains of many of them were never found.

Whenever there was an air raid, the boy had been told, he should head for the nearest river, which would be a natural protection against fire. This occasion was no exception. "When I had found the strength to stand," he recalls, "I remembered that instruction."

Soon he was running westward to the Tenma River, and on the way he saw a procession of people whose skin had been liquified just like his own, and was peeling from their arms and hands. One such victim, however, was a boy about his own age who was lying helpless on the charred ground crying for his mother.

"Get up!" Takahashi cried out. "Come to the river with me!"

The boy did, and was later treated and saved. It is widely thought that by giving him the inspiration to move from the swirling smoke and heat, Takahashi probably saved his life.

He himself was many years recovering from his injuries, though his bent hand, the nerve pain from his burns, and bouts of chronic hepatitis, have stayed with him for life. Nonetheless, he eventually found work as a clerk in the city records department and married. The severe effects of radiation, he thinks, were probably responsible for his being unable to father children.

Understandably, for most of his life he was bitter, especially when he remembered that of the 60 friends, gathered in the school yard that day, only 11 survived. "I always believed," he says, "that the war could have ended without the use of a bomb. That bomb, remember, mostly killed and maimed innocent civilians."

As the years have matured him, however, and he learned to use his right hand again and refocus his daily life around his ailments, he has begun to feel differently. In 1979, he became director of the city's Peace Memorial Museum; in 1983 he was appointed director of the enterprise division of the Hiroshima Peace Culture Foundation, one of several groups that aids victims of the disaster and keeps it alive in the minds of people across the globe.

In this capacity he once entertained, in the small house he and his wife occupy on the city's edge, an NBC television crew that arrived to make a film about Hiroshima specifically for American viewers. "In our own way," a producer told him, "and by making this film, we are really here to say how sorry we are that this awful thing happened."

Takahashi smiled. "I felt so much better," he reflects. "At last the world was listening to the message of the dead." And he adds, "My hope is that this exhibition, 'War and Peace,' will be viewed by as many young people as possible because it is they who must bequeath details of the bombing to the generation that follows them. When we older folks are gone, it will be up to young people everywhere to hand down details of this particularly tragic element of World War II. More than this, it will be up to them to see that it never happens again."

In from the cold

February 22, 1992

THE CRACKLE OF APPLAUSE in the Odawara restaurant the other night was for good-natured Taiko Yoshino, 50, who had finally come home. Had you met Yoshi, as he is known, before he left, you would never have suspected that he was anything other than a one-time prizefighter or an arm wrestler. He was corpulent, yet muscular, with big shoulders that sloped down from where his neck once was. His face was round, and his eyes twinkled incessantly like crystal lights from behind big glasses.

All that was 700 ice-cold showers ago in a mountain retreat in Nakayama, which nestles in the mountains near Chiba, and where biting winds cut mercilessly across the Sea of Japan from Siberia. Now, as he seated himself at the long, low dinner table, he was lean and diamond-faced, and sported a wispy, black beard. His feet were blistered and cracked from walking barefoot in the snow. His gray eyes were heavy with fatigue.

Yoshi is a Buddhist priest of the Nichiren sect, and he had just spent 100 days in what is called *aragyo*, which takes human endurance almost to its limit. During this winter training, he, and the 160 priests with him, subjected themselves to extreme sensory discomfort that ran close to torture: three hours of cold, shallow sleep nightly, if they were lucky, and, to make them thankful for small mercies, meals that existed of a single

144

bowl of rice. They then spent 16 hours chanting sutras and taking those ice-cold showers — seven of them daily — to keep themselves alert.

At nights, Yoshi shivered in his futon, and that was by choice, too. Before leaving, he bought himself a big, mountaineer's sleeping bag from the L.L. Bean catalogue, but only used it for three days. "It made me too warm," he says, "and that meant the first cold shower of each new morning was much harder to bear."

So painful is aragyo that priests often contemplate escaping it. They rarely do, though, for it is this temptation that each must fight. Thus, by exercising such extreme psychological discipline against enormous physical pain, Yoshi, who was born in Aomori Prefecture, and who grew up in Yokosuka, where his father served as a Japanese naval officer, reaffirmed his belief that what he had been doing for more than half his life had been right, and that he should continue it.

And so strong is the element of self-deprivation — or self-inflicted suffering — that one high priest, Nichiryu Abe, proved his inner strength to sustain his life's work by taking up a knife and cutting off the little finger of his left hand. A stocky, ruddy-faced man with an impressive white beard, Abe was one of the visitors to Yoshi's Enmyoji Nichiren Temple, in Odawara, that afternoon. There, in bright sunshine, about 400 friends and followers turned out to welcome their priest home. Before he had time to shower and drink a cup of hot, green tea, however, Yoshi was ceremoniously ridding evil spirits from all who knelt before him, and prescribing good luck.

Outside in the gravel-covered temple yard, other

temple members sipped saké and munched on raw fish. Yoshi, however, his religious ceremonies completed, waited to eat in the restaurant — with 20 of the priests who had endured aragyo with him. It was his first "proper" meal since the ordeal had begun.

Wait! That's not exactly right. In Tokyo Station, on his way back from Nakayama, he had bought himself a ¥750 ramen. "But I didn't eat it all," he remembers. "I couldn't wait to catch the next train down to Odawara."

He and the other men sat on a communal tatami and enjoyed a feast. Yoshi nibbled tentatively on fried prawns, cooked meats, and salads, and sipped a small glass of beer. Two geisha, meanwhile, flitted from priest to priest, pouring drinks and telling jokes. Toasts were drunk. Some of the men lit cigarettes and leaned back, smiling contentedly. Others, spurred on by the geisha, sang enka songs to tunes that poured from the karaoke machine.

Like Yoshi, these priests are exceptional beings who, during aragyo, do what few ordinary people could ever hope to. "But," he said of his colleagues, his voice hoarse from chanting, "we all go through it successfully."

All except one priest, that is. He spent nearly half the 100 days flat on his back, exhausted. But even he was determined to stay— to meditate.

Nichiryu Abe, who led the priests through this winter's aragyo, says it is an absolutely essential experience, but that going through it once is insufficient. Only after about 1,000 days of it — that's 7,000 ice-cold showers and 16,000 hours of chanting and meditating — can a priest even remotely know who he is, he says;

then, and only then, will he be aware of his strengths and weaknesses, and finally be equipped to eliminate the pain and suffering from the lives of his temple members.

Yoshi agrees. As he neared the restaurant, he recalled the 600 days of aragyo already behind him. "They have given me a god-mind," he joked. Just before shambling off to bed, however, he was reminded of the 400 days that were left for him to do. "I look forward to them," he said, his leaden eyes shining with determination. "They will make me a better man."

Wasting not is wanting not

February 15, 1992

WHENEVER ANYONE TELLS you that the Japanese are absolute copiers and not inventors, simply tell them that inventions usually spring from ingenuity and the ability to conserve, and in Japan, there is a tradition of both of these. No one, of course, would hand Japan a medal for environmental conservation after having seen its beaches, or the forest wastelands it has created throughout much of Asia in its pursuit of wood for chopsticks, but that is another matter. I merely refer to Japan's resourcefulness, the necessity for which has been inspired by frugal times.

About 20 years ago, Prince Philip, Duke of Edinburgh, enlightened Britain about the very simple matter of water wastage, when he said, "We urinate a pint or less — then use four gallons to flush it away." The Brits laughed, of course, but the Japanese took his words seriously and responded by installing little spouts atop toilet cisterns that invite us to wash our hands in the water we are, at that moment, sending into the toilet bowl. In this way, of course, the water is being given a dual use.

So is the heat generated when the furnaces, near my home in Higashi-Totsuka, burn the local garbage. I was surprised the other day to learn that it is being used to warm the local swimming pool. It may not be environmentally acceptable, of course, but it is, nonetheless, an inexpensive source of power — and an ingenious way of finding a use for it.

Talking of this, in the city of Beppu, near Oita, on Kyushu, steam heat that is generated by the many hundreds of onsen there is funneled into dozens of local greenhouses, thus enabling market gardeners to grow vegetables and flowers in the heart of winter.

Meanwhile, most of us are aware of municipal efforts to recycle newsprint. Also in Higashi-Totsuka, for 50 or so newspapers left for collection outside an apartment door, private recyclers in Yokohama deliver a package of toilet paper rolls. A lot of conservation, however, is left to the people themselves. The Japanese, as I'm sure you will have noticed, are famous for saving energy by heating or lighting only those rooms of a home they are either using or are about to use. Sometimes, they heat very small areas — thus was born the kotatsu, which apparently provides enough warmth beneath a low table to satisfy a group of people. To benefit, however, all must sit on the floor, a feat I find increasingly difficult to perform, and one that as uncomfortable as it is, nonetheless brings the Japanese family together.

Anyway, this business of conserving truly is a Japanese tradition, and at no time was it more ingenious than during World War II, which, admittedly, brought out the best in peoples across the world. It caught on particularly well, however, in war-ravaged Japan, and much of the resourcefulness born then, and there, has since become folklore.

Lacking metals for radio sets, hinges, and door handles, the Japanese made them from waste fibers. Lacking felt for hats and purses, they manufactured them from a mixture of seaweed and ground peanut shells. Lacking leather for shoes and belts, they processed fish skins and made *them* do. Lacking wool, they made clothes and blankets from something like it that was woven from soybeans. Lacking enough steel to manufacture phonographic needles, they simply made them out of bamboo, and found that they worked quite well.

That's not the end of it. When they did not have enough rice with which to make saké, they simply brewed a wine that passed for it — from acorns. Without sufficient iron for bicycles, they made them from fiber or cardboard. And when they began to run out of gasoline, they made a combustion engine that was fueled by charcoal.

Nor was the kitchen spared from pragmatic conservation, and a lot of this is still being demonstrated today. As a small boy, I remember, I helped my mother by ripping the leaves of cabbages and cutting them from their stems, which were then tossed away. Actually, I ate a few of those stems because, I sensed, they might be good for me, and the Japanese would agree. They cook every part of a cabbage, as they do the shoots of spinach and Brussels sprouts. In some parts of the country, they even use the pods of peas in soup.

And whereas Westerners eat only the pulp of a pumpkin, usually in pies, the Japanese boil, bake, or fry the skin or the shell, then serve it with meat. Like the Chinese, they have also introduced the leaves of certain flowers into salads — chrysanthemums, for example — and think nothing of finding some way of serving all of a fish without throwing any of it away, except the bones.

The nearest Westerners come to anything like this, I seem to recall, is boiling the carcasses of chickens and turkeys to make soup, and turning dandelions, those awful weeds that invade lawns, into wine. Maybe something can be learned from the frugal, conservation-conscious Japanese.

The run-around

December 15, 1990

ALL ALAN CHIVERS wanted was to settle in Japan for a couple of years — to learn Japanese so he would be able to converse more deeply with his girlfriend, Mayumi, whom he had met a few years back while he was driving a fork-lift truck in Sydney, Australia. "But," he says ruefully, "life's simple things aren't always that simple at all."

A quietly-spoken 23-year-old from Avon, England, Alan arrived in Tokyo in October 1989, on a three-month tourist visa, and immediately applied for a student visa so he could attend a Japanese language school. When his application was refused — with no reason given — he began a bureaucratic run-around that set him thinking: "If everyone at Immigration didn't complicate things, they wouldn't have to do any overtime."

Alan quickly found part-time work teaching English to raise money in case he had to leave Japan quickly, but, last December, he successfully applied to have his tourist visa extended for another three months. "I'm really serious about learning Japanese," he reiterated to officials. Then, in February, he applied for a working visa. But he was again refused without a reason, and given three weeks to leave the country.

Before going, Alan applied for the visa once more — this time under the sponsorship of a Roppongi coffee shop owner who said he would hire him as an ¥800-yen-an-hour waiter so he would at least be able to pay the rent on his room while attending school. The application was refused because Alan did not have a university degree. "I didn't think a university degree was necessary to serve coffee," he says.

Of course, he could have bought a fake degree like a lot of other people I know, but preferred not to cheat. "If I get found out," he said, "I'll really be up the creek."

With his money running out, his only option now was to buy a ¥150,000 one-way air ticket back to Australia, where he knew he'd find work, and this he did — in April. He loaded trucks in a publisher's warehouse in Sydney to make enough money to pay his way back to Tokyo — and another three-month visa. Mayumi, meanwhile, a Tokyo model agency coordinator, applied for a student visa on Alan's behalf. But the year's quota on foreign students had now been filled, she was told, and Alan would have to apply after October.

Last June, having spent all his Australian-earned savings on another ¥150,000 one-way air fare to Tokyo, Alan resumed his part-time teaching job. And in August — after reiterating to Immigration officials, "I'm here to learn Japanese" — he got another extension.

But his life couldn't continue like this. "I was fed up with the run-around, the stays of execution," he says. So in September he decided to make his final pitch for a student visa. "If it doesn't pan out this time," he told friends, "I'll forget the whole bloody thing."

As he'd done before, he completed a form and attached to it a letter explaining why he wanted to study

Japanese. He also attached eight photographs, a certificate of health, a "personal history," his passport, his high school diploma (which he had to have translated into Japanese), and proof that he had ¥1 million — money sent to him by his parents — in a Japanese bank account. All was set, and Alan Chivers waited to hear from Immigration via his Japanese language school.

Two weeks ago, the call finally came. Alan now had a student visa! The story, however, does not rest here. Under new regulations adopted last August he must be airborne once more. Only a Japanese immigration authority *outside* the country is legally allowed to staple the visa, now in his wallet, to a page in his passport. He could, of course, fly to Seoul, or Hong Kong, have his visa stapled there, then catch the next flight back. But since that would cost him ¥100,000 he's decided to pay an extra ¥50,000 — to spend Christmas in England with Mayumi.

In April, when Alan attends Japanese classes, he will have endured a bureaucratic paper chase which, with visa and transportation costs — not to mention other expenses like his medical examination, translation fees, and time lost from work — began almost a million yen ago.

"But it's not just the cash," he says. "If they'd given me a visa at the start it would have saved me a helluva lot of heartache. Not only that, I'd probably already be speaking quite a bit of Japanese by now."

The bar that Sato built

September 22, 1990

LIFE BEGAN ALL OVER again for Kazu Sato, 37, the day he quit his job at Ikebukuro's Metropolitan Hotel to run a little conversation bar called Mickey House. "As a salaryman," he says, "you can't make money. Your income is fixed. You might get a raise with time, but you generally make the same money, year in, year out, however hard you work. Now I work for me, and the sky is my limit."

And work he has. On any Friday or Saturday night, Mickey House, an unpretentious, L-shaped little bar on the fourth floor of a building near Wendy's in Takadanobaba — with its carpetless, checker-board linoleum floor, fold-up tables, and bench seats — is packed out. Or as Sato says, "It is wall to wall people with hardly any space to breathe."

A man who once resigned himself to serving a dignified clientele of industrialists and executives in crisp white shirts and business suits, Kazu Sato now satisfies one which wears sweat shirts and jeans, and, for the most part, is under 30. "And I'm happier for it," he says. "Where else can I enjoy the company of young people from all over the world in just a few square meters of floor space?"

The transition in his life came suddenly, just a few months ago. Until then, he had been a customer at the bar's forerunner: an eight-year-old language center that served drinks and food, and which was owned by the proprietor of a Japanese language school. But business there was not good — not even during the three years or so it was run by a new manager. Something was missing. "There were times," Sato reflects, "when I was the only guy in the place." He had a hard time understanding why — especially as he stared out through the large picture window that let in the flickering lights of throbbing Takadanobaba.

Last January, however, all that changed. When he heard that the owner was contemplating closing the business for good, his sentiments got the better of him. "I'll buy it," he said impulsively. And that's exactly what he did. "I didn't want to lose this place," he reflects fondly. "I didn't want it to disappear. When I was a salaryman, this was my oasis. This is where I relaxed after work over a cold beer. This where I could be quiet when I wanted to, and meet new foreign friends."

All that is history now. Sato handed in his notice at the Metropolitan Hotel, where he had risen from a waiter in the tea room, then in the coffee shop, to become assistant manager of the Sky Lounge, then of the exclusive Membership Club, and, on February 1, breathed new life into Mickey House. He opened it as one of the growing number of Tokyo conversation bars, and, judging by the response, it seems to have be come something of an institution. Reason? "Simple," says one of the customers, Koji Yoshida, a student. "No one gets ripped off."

Nor was Kazu Sato when he bought the place. He struck a deal with the owner to buy the business for a meager ¥4 million, payable over time, when or if the business worked out. A further expense is his monthly rent — ¥175,000 payable to the landlady, who lives upstairs and who never complains about the noise, particularly when the Friday and Saturday night customers decide that instead of conversing, they want to sing and dance.

But already, Sato is grossing ¥300,000 a week, and, as news of his venture spreads, it promises to pull in even more. The money is not all his, though. Apart from the rent and a business loan, he has a partner: an equally gregarious entrepreneur named Shawn Barton, 29, who hails from Bedford, England.

"We work well as a team," Sato says. They do, and, in so doing have given Mickey House an atmosphere all its very own. "I guess I like people and languages," Sato adds.

He was born in the ski resort of Manza, the son of a post office accountant, and was educated in Hampstead, England. He later studied German in Zurich, Switzerland, and, while working as a waiter-porter in a bed and breakfast establishment in nearby Zermatt, was able to add a smattering of French and Italian.

Secretly, he always wanted a business of his own, and one in which he could practice what he had already picked up. "At the Metropolitan Hotel," he says, "I couldn't even use my English. All the wealthy Japanese, the company presidents, only ever spoke their own language."

That was another reason be made his bid for Mickey House. It is far — very far — from the luxury Sato knew at the Membership Club. While this charges a ¥100,000 initiation fee, plus a ¥400,000 deposit, and an annual membership fee of ¥23,000, Mickey House lets its foreign clients in free and asks its Japanese customers, mostly young men and women office workers and students, to pay a mere ¥600.

More to the customers' liking is that once inside the little place, coffee and tea is free, a soft drink is only ¥300, and beer and hard liquor ¥400. On Saturday nights, however — Party Night — the Japanese pay ¥1,500 and the foreigners ¥1,000. But both these entrance fees include one free drink and a light meal, a slice of pizza, perhaps, or a shrimp *au gratin*. "We're trying to provide an honest, moderately priced night out for people who want to meet others and practice their languages," Sato says.

Just as the local people go there to try their English, so the foreigners stop by to try their Japanese. In recent weeks, though, Sato and Barton have noticed that more and more customers seated at the little tables are from Taiwan, Malaysia, China, and Singapore. Many others are speaking German, French, and Italian.

No wonder, then, that customers poured into Mickey House recently to watch World Cup soccer on the bar's TV. To make sure they were not disappointed, the owners recorded games on the VCR when they were telecast "live" via the bar's satellite dish in the night, then played them the following day.

At any given time on a typical weekday night, however, 30 people have dropped in, and of these, about 10 are university and college students who have sought out a congenial site for their homework. At Mickey House, after all, there is always a song in the tape deck, or a song in Sato's heart. "Or a new person to introduce to the group," Sato says quickly. "We are all friends here. We make sure that everyone who comes in here is never left out. That is our motto, and nothing will ever change it."

Thank you, Sir
March 30, 1991

AND NOW FOR SOMETHING completely different — a letter from one of those Westerners who have been in Japan so long, they are very definitely a part of it. It not only gave me insights into the writer, but myself, too. It was 21 type-written pages long, and it espoused many ways in which I could improve the quality of my life. "This letter, long overdue, is to say hello to you," it says. "Consider it a fan letter if you like. I am not out to kill you, as you say some letter writers are. They either praise you, or want to kill you."

The writer went on to say that he had savored, stored, and remembered each of my columns since they began appearing a year or so ago, and, as I prepared to leave Japan, he was inspired to tell me so. "Thank you," he says, "for taking up the cause of minorities."

Let me give you a profile of the writer. He is Norwegian-born Per Winther who, at 58, looks back on a life of action and intrigue. I have never met him, but wish I had. He is yet someone else after my own heart: a traveler, a collector, an artist, a conservationist, and a man who values his family. Like I did, he grew up during World War II. Then, at 18, he joined the Merchant Marine. Five years later, he saw India and satisfied a dream — to spend a night, lit by a full moon, at the Taj Mahal. The trouble was that he fell asleep on the wrong side of huge, iron gates and, after they had been locked by the night watchman, had to scale a high wall to get out. While doing this he sprained his ankle, but it was worth the inconvenience. There is nothing quite like satisfying a dream — is there? — no matter how crazy some people may consider it.

Somewhere along the road, Per Winther studied yoga, became a vegetarian, and married a Japanese woman who bore him a daughter and a son. He has lived in Japan since 1988, and has interested himself in wood carving, which he studied with the Ainu in Hokkaido. He later made pipes for smokers, even though he doesn't smoke himself, and bags and book covers for his friends. Most of these were cut and sewn from secondhand leather, primarily old luggage and women's high boots — so as to reduce the need to slaughter any more animals than necessary.

Some while ago, one of Per Winther's students gave him a leather jacket that he, in turn, had been given by someone else 20 years before. Winther turned it into a purse. In this respect he says that when he read, in one of my earlier columns, that my briefcase had finally given up life, he was sorry it had to be cast into the garbage. He would have liked it. "I know one-hundred percent," he says, "that I could have made something interesting out of it." He also says he could never understand why a reader should have criticized this column, or the one in which I lamented the high cost of coffee.

Per Winther tries not to drink coffee claiming that, like meat, it is unhealthy. In fact, he says, we must all be careful about what we eat and drink lest it should affect our minds, and in this respect meat is probably the worst food there is. "It is secondhand food," he says, "because you also get the animal's toxins."

He is doubtless right in all he says. On the matter of food and drink, though, he and I differ. I enjoy a sirloin steak more than anything, and, as I have written, I could spend my entire life in coffee shops, reading poetry.

Finally, says Per Winther, he would like to analyze my hand-writing, for he is also a certified master graphoanalyst. "Even just your signature would tell a few things," he says.

Thank you for writing to me so thoughtfully, kindly, and in so much detail, Sir. Maybe one day I will shake your hand and tell you how I, too, saw India when I was 18, how I too like to paint and carve wood, and how I share your views on the joy of the family — and that, as I have also said in a previous column, political parties don't rule, but govern. You should be aware of one thing, though: that English-language newspapers published by the Japanese in Japan are precisely just that. By no stretch of the imagination can they be compared with Western newspapers as we know them. Hence governments here "rule" and people never simply die, but "pass away."

I am sorry you suffered the indignity of being ejected from the old Sanno Hotel because you then sported a beard. And on this point, I speak with some authority. Back in 1957, I was offered my first job as a newspaper reporter on condition that I shaved a little goatee that had taken me several years to grow. I did so because in those days I was eager and hungry. But I would never do this today. Not for anyone.

Again, Sir, thank you.

Be on your guard

April 20, 1991

SOME LITTLE WHILE AGO, a man my wife met on the train invited us to his house for dinner — to seek our advice about his pending vacation in Quebec, the French-speaking province of Canada. Was it true, he asked, that if he did not put a $1 bill under his pillow every night, the maid would refuse to make his bed? I assured him it wasn't. I also said that this kind of nonsense is usually perpetrated by travel agents seeking to ensure that the Japanese show the world a polite and generous face. He then began asking me about tipping, ordering cabs and meals, and speaking French.

The entire experience not only convinced me that many Japanese are somehow ill-equipped to travel the world, but inspired me to help them by addressing some of the questions my new Japanese friend raised. In so doing, I have put myself in the shoes of the Japanese man or woman who is ardently exploring the big world beyond these shores for the first time.

• Tipping: This is done a lot in the West because many people in the service industry are paid a lower-than-usual wage on the simple assumption that the public will show their appreciation with small gifts of cash. I don't like the idea — which is a cultural quirk of the West — but have got used to it.

The general rule is to give a tip worth about 15

percent of the bill. Under certain circumstances, however, if the service is particularly good, or the waitress or waiter has performed a special service, it is acceptable to pay up to 20 percent.

This part of travel, however, is insignificant compared with the dangers.

• While it is usually unnecessary — and culturally vulgar — to count change in Japan, it is most certainly necessary to do so in the West. While few people will ever try to cheat, mistakes do occur. A quick calculation of change is not a bad idea.

• Muggings in some large Western cities are on the increase and "rich" tourists, particularly the Japanese, are obvious targets. So, they should never carry large amounts of money on them unless it is absolutely necessary.

It is well known that the Japanese travel to vacation destinations for a very few days at a time, and with more cash in their wallets or purses than most Westerners ever have. When strolling out for dinner, or doing small-scale, casual shopping, a good tip — and one I always follow myself — is to carry a relatively small amount of cash (say, about $20) and a credit card. A stolen credit card is useless. At least, all it takes to inactivate one is a phone call. An argument, struggle, or fight over a walletful of money can be lethal.

• Many of the things that endear foreigners to Japan do not apply in the West. It is too risky, for instance, to leave a purse or a coat unattended there. Women in Japan think nothing of leaving a handbag on a restaurant table for as long as it takes to make a phone call or use the toilet. In a large North American or European city, however, they would be taking a risk of having their belongings stolen.

• When in the streets of a large city, think ahead. Anticipate. I do — all the time. Remember that crime is fueled by poverty, and this is something about which Japan knows little. In cities like New York and Los Angeles, where neighbors steal from each other, a lot of people are driven to crime out of absolute necessity. It is a shocking sign of our times.

So keep away from rowdy nightspots that are frequented by poorer people. And remember some of the ploys:

• While many impoverished Westerners cannot bring themselves to mug, they nonetheless employ other, less violent tactics. One of the latest is to carry a cheap bottle of wine and to contrive to collide with a tourist and drop it — "Hey, mister! You made me drop my liquor. D'you realise that was an expensive bottle of scotch? Gimme $100 — now!"

• Avoid any kind of body contact in the streets, not only for this reason, but to make it harder for pickpockets.

Having said all this, I should add that the people in any small town or village in any Western country are as kind, helpful, and honorable as the gentle Japanese themselves. I have heart-rending stories to tell of my travels abroad but will save them for another time.

Meanwhile, when the Japanese venture to another country, they should be on their guard.

A dirty business
May 11, 1991

THERE IS SOMETHING distinctly rotten in the state of Japan's air travel industry, and few people, if any, are doing anything about it. Most of us, of course, dislike the recent fare increases, but accept them as a part of inflation. The business of which people are to be permitted to be passengers on what flights, however, is entirely another matter. And the scandal here is unique to Japan.

It is two-fold. First, airlines that have landing and takeoff rights at New Tokyo International Airport are not always eager to honor tickets — most of them return tickets — that have been bought abroad, and this leaves a lot of passengers wondering, worrying, scrambling for help and information, and convinced that the business is corrupt. The second problem occurs at Japanese vacation times. National airlines prefer not to sell tickets to those people wanting to leave Tokyo for such attractive destinations as, say, Bangkok, Hong Kong, or Singapore — either alone or part of a family — because they know that they can pack one plane after another to such destinations with huge groups of Japanese tourists.

Think of the enormous turn-around! Think of the huge profits the airlines are making at the expense of the Japanese people who, not knowing any better, are willing to pay the world's highest fares to visit far-away places for only five days or so at a time.

If the Japanese are naive enough to pay good money to see the United States, Canada, or Timbuktu for five days, it is *their* problem. By exploiting them, however — or by not honoring return tickets bought abroad, or those tickets for holiday trips — the airlines and their agents are operating outside the industry's international laws and ethics.

For all this, discrimination exists unchallenged — as borne out by the ticket classifications that exist within Japan's airlines:

- Fully paid and bought in Japan. Top priority
- Discount and bought in Japan. Second priority
- Fully paid but bought abroad. Third priority
- Discount but bought abroad. Fourth priority

So, if you hold a valid ticket that is at the bottom of this pile, don't be surprised if a travel agent tells you that there are no available seats, particularly if you want to go to a place that is popular with Japanese travelers. Chances are, there are *plenty* of seats still to be sold, but that the airlines have told the agent to sell them only to Japanese groups, and to put other prospective passengers on a waiting list.

This happened to my wife and I when we tried to make flight arrangements for Bangkok last April and Singapore at Christmas. On both occasions we started trying to book a flight many weeks before and struck one obstacle after another — until we met a travel agent in Takadanobaba who was honest enough to tell us exactly *why* he couldn't make reservations to Bangkok on our behalf.

"I've been told only to sell them to Japanese traveling in groups," he said, "or individuals who buy package tours." He nonetheless promised to let us know if some seats remained unsold and assured us that they would be offered to us first. Meanwhile, we waited anxiously, and wondered if we should change our travel plans.

To be fair, the agent eventually *did* call us. He had booked a departure flight for us, but could not guarantee our return. By then, however — when time had almost run out — we had finally been able to buy tickets to Bangkok and back, thanks to The Japan Times Travel Bureau, whose staff did some extra work on our behalf.

Discrimination is only one part of the problem, though. Japan's air travel industry is further darkened by the way it fixes prices. Air tickets bought here are the most expensive in the world because airlines prefer not to use the current yen-dollar rate — the one that the rest of us have to abide by, whether we like it or not — but a rate set by the Japanese government several years ago at the request of Japan Air Lines.

Take a deep breath. The rate used by the Japanese travel industry is, in fact, around ¥250 to the U.S. dollar, depending on that day's monetary market. And by anyone's standard, this is little more than theft. Actually, when you compare the service JAL offers with that given on other international airlines, it might also be considered money obtained under false pretenses.

All is not well in the air travel industry here. It is time it cleaned house.

Human bondage

April 4, 1992

THIS, AND THE OTHER stories I am about to tell you this week, is not a happy one. Ten years ago, and within only one month, two separate doctors told Yuriko H. that both her parents were terminally ill — her mother with a serious lung ailment, her father with oral cancer. The depth of the predicament that was about to unfold for her is, it seems, the predicament of all too many Japanese women who would like to complain about it, but cannot find the proper words to do so.

Because Yuriko, then 22, was the only daughter, she was expected to refocus her life, and nurse both her parents until their deaths, whenever that time would come. I tell her story this week because when I told it to three different women recently, all said, "But this is very common in Japan. Almost the same thing happened to me."

No one, of course, denies that sick parents must be nursed. I would have nursed mine. But why, these women ask themselves, should the job automatically fall upon them? Shouldn't such severe family problems be shared? I, in turn, ask why it is that a society expects the women it so readily suppresses to accept such responsibility alone, and in their best years.

"My problem," says Yuriko, "has always been trying to find someone who is prepared to shoulder some of the burden — just to give me the time to read a book or write a letter to a friend." She should know about this. The moment she knew she had to tend her parents, her boyfriend ended their four-year relationship, and she gave up all hopes of a career as a librarian, settling instead for a job as a waitress that would enable her to leave work at 5 p.m. each day so she could rush home and prepare supper for her parents by 6 p.m.

For 10 years, she accepted no evening commitments except her weekly English lesson — a lesson she began taking in June in the ardent hope that one day, she might break free of her human bondage and turn her life around before it was too late.

Last August, as his cancer worsened and spread, her father was taken to hospital and was not expected to leave. To save him, doctors removed most of his tongue and part of his jaw. Yuriko spent time rushing back and forth between his bed in a Tokyo hospital and the family's home in suburban Yokohama — to bathe her mother, now bedridden, cook for her, and read to her. Her mother died just before Christmas, while, on the suggestion of a former university classmate who offered to fill in for her, Yuriko prepared to take her first-ever vacation as an adult — a five-day group excursion to Hawaii.

She canceled her trip, of course, and, meanwhile, her father left hospital and seemed to gain strength. The last I heard, he was so frustrated with not being able to speak properly that he was beating Yuriko with a garden rake he keeps beside the refrigerator. When I spoke to her the other night, Yuriko broke down and said, "My life is ruined. I have nothing. The boyfriends I once had refused to come near the house because they couldn't bear to look at my ailing parents. Because I couldn't offer them a future away from what I had to suffer through, I lost contact with them. Now I see no end."

One of the women to whom I mentioned this is Tomoko S., of Atami. Hers is a frighteningly similar experience, lightened by her philosophical view of fate and how to await it. Her parents had been ailing for 20 years, her diabetic father with circulatory and respiratory problems, her mother with angina. "Helping my parents," she says resiliently, "has brought me my greatest joy. I can honestly say that I have done my best." But, she adds, "I would have liked to have been married through all this and had a family of my own — and at least a husband to help and support me."

She, too, discovered that the men she met were not mentally equipped to help shoulder her burden — except one, that is. He was a wealthy, understanding American cattle rancher she had met when she was in her mid-30s. He visited her frequently, staying at the four-room house she shared with her parents, and paid helpers to take over so she could spend the odd week with him at his Oklahoma home. Two years ago, and despite his age — 64 — he was preparing to move to Japan to give Tomoko the help he thought she needed on a constant basis — with the cooking, shopping, and cleaning. But things were not to be.

Last July, Tomoko's father died suddenly of a heart attack, and the shock of his death caused her mother to suffer a fierce stroke that left her completely paralyzed down the left side of her body and unable to speak. Then, in September, Tomoko's American friend died unexpectedly of the liver cancer he never knew he had. Her little life had caved in. "One thing I knew," she recalls, "was that things had to get better because they couldn't have got any worse."

Today, she spends her days tending her mother's every need, and, to put food on the table, teaches English in the evenings to high school dropouts who don't particularly want to learn it. She does not complain.

Nor does Nobuko R. She's 42 today, and finally free of having to nurse an alcoholic father who lost his legs when he fell under a train, and a mother who suffered a succession of nervous breakdowns, one of which left her permanently psychotic. Her father died three years ago, her mother in January. Nobuko's seven-year ordeal of looking after them had ended. She now works as an executive secretary at a British securities company — the same firm, in fact, that understood her personal problems and hired her part-time so she would be able to deal with them.

All these women, however, have something else in common. They each have no sisters but a brother. Nobuko's offered some help, like staying with his parents when his sister needed a break. But Yuriko's brother, who is 23, and who has not worked since dropping out of school when he was 16, has not done anything, even though he lives in the same house. In fact, he recently became so used to seeing his father strike Yuriko with the garden rake handle that he began to do the same thing himself.

"Some nights," Yuriko says solemnly, "I cook for the family, do the washing, make sure there's a film in the VCR, then lock myself in my room so no one can harm me. After that, when I hear my father go to his room, I try to sleep myself."

Tomoko, meanwhile, talks of a married brother who told her that the problem of looking after sick parents had to be exclusively hers because, after all, she was a woman. After a while, bitter family arguments ensued, not only between Tomoko and her brother, but between Tomoko and her sister-in-law who said she did not want to raise her children in a house tainted with sickness. Tomoko replied that if she could be so lucky as to one day have children, she would be perfectly happy to raise them anywhere — "So long as there was lots of love around and plenty of understanding that some people, like my parents, weren't so fortunate as other people."

In the past eight years, she has spoken to her brother and sister-in-law once. That was at her father's funeral, when they wanted to discuss his will.

"I don't care about that any more," Tomoko says. "I just want to be happy, and make my mother happy for the time she has left with me."

Adds Yuriko: "I know in my heart that looking after my parents was something I had to do because it was expected of me. But there were times when I wished I'd had some kind of moral, if not practical, support to help me through some very difficult times."

Let the sun set

September 29, 1990

YOU MAY BELIEVE WHAT I am about to tell you. You may not *want* to believe it. But it is true, nonetheless — two grown men talking about virginity, of all things, while making moral judgments on vacationing Japanese women.

One of these men is Shintaro Ishihara, who wrote the book *The Japan That Can Say No*. The other is a freelance writer named Hiroshi Yamaguchi. Both claim that Japanese women travel to Guam specifically to have sex with American GIs at the Anderson Air Force Base — Ishihara in the monthly magazine *Chuo Koron*, and Yamaguchi in a column called "Japanese Perspective," which appears in *The Japan Times*, but not, I am happy to tell you, in *The Weekly*.

A recent effort by Yamaguchi — "Japan's sun is sure to set" — was sparked by comments Shintaro Ishihara had made some six months ago. By telling *his* version of what supposedly goes on in Guam, however, where he plays golf, Yamaguchi casts nasty aspersions on a lot of people and dredges up wartime emotions to support arguments against a social problem for which he lacks both the skill and the good taste to properly explain.

Because four-day package tours to Guam cost only about ¥50,000, air fare and accommodation included, he has heard, he says — from Japanese expatriates, no less — that the women flock to "the nearest American territory" specifically to have sex with American GIs.

"I was told," he adds, "that Japanese women like to boast particularly about their liaison with black American GIs."

First, I question the choice of topic for a column in which Yamaguchi purports to offer "a Japanese perspective." (Perspective on what?) Second, it is none of his bloody business who vacationing Japanese women choose to sleep with. And if they *do* happen to enjoy dating blacks, good for them. I would have been a little happier had he made some comment on the vast numbers of Japanese salarymen who leave Tokyo on sex pilgrimages each year, specifically to have sex with prostitutes in Bangkok.

After a meaningless discourse on the Anderson Air Base, which Yamaguchi said he visited in 1968, he tells us about a bomber, the B-52. Just why he does this, we are not quite sure. It makes no point whatsoever, supports no arguments, and has nothing whatsoever to do with either the women he is criticizing, or the men they supposedly meet.

What really bombs, of course, is Yamaguchi's senseless, vulgar, inane, ignorant piece writing, which is an insult not only to women, but to journalism.

"I am not nationalist of the Ishihara type," he tells us. (As if anyone cares.) "However, my heart aches as I think of all those *tokkotai* suicide pilots who chose death to protect their motherland and their loves ones."

More rubbish! Most civilized people see no nobility whatsoever in suicide missions. In fact, my heart has always bled *not* for the pilots who chose to take their own lives, but for the forces who died from their attacks —

in a war that was started, no less, by Japan's senseless, unprovoked bombing of Pearl Harbor in 1941.

In any case, what in God's name have Japanese suicide pilots of the 1940s got to do with Yamaguchi's "licentious young women" of the 1990s sleeping with black GIs at the Anderson Air Base? If I have missed something, please tell me.

No! Wait! Yamaguchi does it for us.

"Japan's relations with the United States today," he writes, "are troubled by an assortment of conflicts. But in no way can such discords be resolved through hidden merriments on Guam."

Were they ever supposed to be? Yamaguchi concludes his piece by implying that if enough Japanese women have sex with foreigners, particularly American airmen, "the sun will set on Japan" sooner than we think. What he means, of course, is that Japan will cease to be what it has always sought to be — a pure-blooded race. Well, if that's all it is going to take for the rising sun to go down, let it sink I say.

With ingredients like those you have read, you might think that Yamaguchi's column would be a sure-fire winner, if only for its outlandishness. It won't be, though. He writes badly, is insulting, and suffers acutely from a lack of clarity of thought, which is where all good writing begins.

I am left wondering how this kind of mush could ever be assigned, bought, even translated from the Japanese, let alone published. After all, to get something so irresponsible as this printed in a big-city newspaper like *The Japan Times* — on a business page, no less! — you would really have to know someone who could vouch for your ability, even when you had none, and order any editors who might oppose what you had written, to use it anyway.

If you *didn't* know anyone, what you had written would end up where it belonged — in the trash can.

Maybe, when we come to think of it, the sun should set on Hiroshi Yamaguchi.

• *Author's note: While some Japanese magazines continued to print Yamaguchi's racist comments, he was quickly dropped from The Japan Times shortly after this column appeared. I like to think I had something to do with it.*

Japan's Dutch paradise

April 11, 1992

SIPPING A COLD BEER under a warm March sun, while waiting for a pleasure barge at a canal boat station, I learned the true meaning of "cultural exchange" and how, despite its suspicion of the outside world, Japan unabashedly reaches across oceans to adopt another country's lifestyle. In front of me, beyond the turquoise water, lay a bank of crimson tulips, and behind me, a windmill turned in a soft breeze.

As the big town clock struck two, the silence of a golden day was broken further by the clatter of horses' hooves on gray, cobblestones, and a small entourage of women scurried by in wooden clogs.

Was this Holland? Or Japan?

It was both, for I had come to a place called Huis Ten Bosch, where time stands still, as time often should for busy people.

To most ears, the very name is curious indeed, and does not somehow belong in Japan. But it is suitable nonetheless. Huis Ten Bosch (pronounced "House Ten Boss" and meaning "home in the woods,") is the Dutch royal palace in the Hague, and here, on a 1.5 million square-meter site strewn against tranquil Omura Bay on the southwestern-most tip of Kyushu, it has been uncannily reproduced, bathroom for bathroom, staircase for staircase.

So has the best of Holland's built heritage in general.

It has been reincarnated in the stalwart Dutch architectural styles of the past four centuries and, somehow, with the imprint of the noble Dutch spirit. Thus Huis Ten Bosch is a composite of Holland's most distinguished old-world architecture, a collage of actual public places, so to speak, that still function today — fine old town squares, church spires, stables, and narrow, windings streets, and all were "transplanted" after having been carefully studied from photographs and civic plans, by architects, builders, and historians from both countries.

The result fools even the Dutch themselves. "It is like being in Holland and walking through the ideal city just after it had been built," said a young Dutch jeweler I met there. "It is like walking back through history — to the very beginning, before fine buildings gathered the soot that made them even finer."

More of a miracle is that two years ago, no one thought that anyone could ever build anything useful on this land, let alone create a piece of Europe there. "It was a desert," Paul S. Takada, managing director of the parent company, Nagasaki Holland Village Company, recalls. "Quite frankly, it was a place nobody wanted."

It was. And it was among the few areas of flatland in the region — land that had been reclaimed from the sea some 12 years before, like most of Holland itself has been over centuries, and earmarked for local industry, perhaps a factory or two. When no industry arrived there, the Nagaaki Prefectural Government made it known that the site was for sale to anyone who would develop it, and it was then that the owners of a theme park called Nagasaki Holland Village, which opened in 1983, decided to buy it and build a similar project 30 km by road away, and south across Omura Bay.

While Huis Ten Bosch is Japan's largest waterfront theme park — more than twice the size of Tokyo's Disneyland, in fact — it is really something more. Work on it started in October 1988. Two-and-a-half years later, it was open for all to see — a magnificent resort-playground for those who can afford to sample Dutch styling at its most luxurious and expensive. Each of the 250 villas that have risen there, all of them equipped with garden-side moorings for yachts and deep-sea cruisers, can be bought for as much as ¥70 million; townhouse-style condominiums cost ¥40 million, though some of these may be rented — for ¥900,000 for 90 days.

The cost of the project to date is almost as unspeakable as it is incalculable: a fat ¥220 billion, which has been amassed by some of Japan's largest corporations, including Kirin Brewery, the Nagasaki Motor Bus Company, Nippon Telegraph and Telephone, Matsushita, and Nippon Steel. Within another two years, when Huis Ten Bosch has been completed to become self-sufficient as a town large enough to accommodate some 30,000 people, it will have cost its 82 shareholders a staggering ¥540 billion.

The so-called "ordinary" folk who may want to visit Huis Ten Bosch casually, for either long or short stays, will be more interested in its five first-class hotels, 53 restaurants jointly satisfying tastes that range from hamburgers to gourmet dishes, 61 specialty shops, the fleets of buses and taxi cabs whose numbers will depend on how many people are using the resort at one given time, and a slew of some 20 attractions, including exhibitions, film shows, parks and gardens, a fitness center, a public marina fashioned after Holland's Leiden Naval Academy, and a canal system that is 6 km long, 20 meters wide, and an average 2.5 meters deep, and serviced by some 41 pleasure boats.

Indeed, Huis Ten Bosch is luxury living at its most eloquent — a truly world-class place. Yet all I knew about it, or most other people, come to that, was contained in a television advertisement that shows British actor Peter O'Toole on a canal boat gliding against a backdrop of gray-pink buildings. All O'Toole says in that advertisement is "Huis Ten Bosch," but it is enough to stir the imagination. Initially, however, I was not enthused about accepting an invitation to visit it.

The occasion was a press preview, four or five days before Netherlands' Queen Beatrix was to visit the site herself, and a week or so before opening day, when, despite heavy rain, about 11,000 people surged in through the main gate to the sounds of 1,500 fireworks, and the gentle lowering of a white bridge that links a replica of Nijenrode Castle, which serves as the entrance building, to the site.

I have never liked media previews, particularly those in Japan. It is a strange phenomenon, indeed, but Japanese journalists have been primed to write what they are told to write, and never to question. So they are handed enough hand-outs to fill a large shopping bag, and it is from these that they build their stories.

For me, however, this information was useless, so I told myself that this visit would be what I made it.

Maybe I could make it different, simply by breaking free of the crowd and wandering off on my own, as I am want to do, and asking questions. That is what I did.

My flight left Tokyo International Airport at 8:30 a.m. and arrived in Nagasaki some two hours later. There, an avalanche of reporters, cameramen, and anyone else who might have been involved in the travel industry — 400 people in all — were shepherded into eight buses that traveled to Huis Ten Bosch in convoy. The silence was deafening. Most of the people on my bus, the first one, were asleep, having risen that day at 5 a.m., like me.

Nearly two hours later, we were on a rugged peninsula of little mountains and outcrops, and shortly after that, our bus drew into the huge parking lot, which has space for 12 buses and 8,000 cars, and the experience that soon unfolded was strange, indeed. As we shambled from our buses through the red-bricked reception area carrying overnight bags, we left behind a rather ugly, unkempt Japanese landscape of shacks, pipes, and broken walls and fences, and had come to a manicured paradise. It was fast approaching noon. The sun shone relentlessly. And I wanted my lunch.

Before this, however, after a brief look at what first confronts the visitor — "Nijenrode Castle" — we were ushered into a cavernous auditorium to watch a film that showed how this little desert was made fertile, and how sturdy trees, and those tulips, would be encouraged to sprout there. Since the film was entirely in Japanese, as well as the lecture afterward, I slipped from the auditorium.

That was when I met the polished, erudite Paul Tanaka who has spent so much time around Dutch workers that he now speaks English with a Dutch accent!

"Well," he said, uncoiling himself from a deep sofa, "what do you think so far?"

"I am overwhelmed," I said.

And I was. I was also a little bemused.

When Tanaka discovered that I was the only Western journalist in the group, and one who could neither speak nor read Japanese, he immediately said, "We must do something about it. Please wait a moment." And he assigned a translator to accompany me wherever I wanted to go.

It was through her, a gifted young woman named Michiyo Hashimura, that I discovered the extent of Huis Ten Bosch's royal tastes. In the Palace, for instance, I marveled at a fine collection of Oriental rugs, and original paintings by many of such Dutch masters as Rembrandt, who fathered a new school of art. There, in this corner of a piece of land that had once been a desert, was one of the finest collections of Flemish paintings I had seen anywhere except, perhaps, at the National Gallery in London.

On that pleasure boat, I remembered how Japan and Holland have been intrinsically entwined for nearly four centuries. The Dutch, after all — together with the Portuguese, who introduced both Roman Catholicism and guns — were among Japan's very first foreigner traders. In 1639, the Portuguese were expelled with their enemies, the Protestant English, and from that moment, Japan's Tokugawa shogunate (military government) ordered a policy of self-imposed isolation, closing all major ports except the one in Nagasaki, and restricted foreign trade to that brought in by the Dutch, and, to a lesser extent, the Chinese and Koreans.

Most of the trading during the ensuing Edo period, which lasted until 1853, was done through the Dutch East India Company's small trading house on tiny Dejima Island, in Nagasaki's deep harbor, and was then distributed throughout other parts of Japan. Dutch ships that sailed from Batavia (now Jakarta), brought such goods as silk, woolen textiles, and glassware, some of the very best there was. They then left for Europe with cargoes of gold, silver, and porcelain.

Especially valuable among these, Japan's very first exports, were such porcelains as Imari and Kakiemon, which came to have a significant influence on Denmark's Royal Copenhagenware, Germany's Meissenware, and Holland's world-famous Deftware.

But trading was only part of the relationship. Numerous Dutch people helped lay the foundations of Japan's modernization. They included Ridder H. van Kattendyke who, as an instructor at the Nagasaki Naval Institute, established at the end of the Edo period, taught basic Western science. Meanwhile, a man named J.L.C Pompe van Meerdevoort, brought and helped develop Western medicine.

Through that open door on Dejima Island, wide-ranging exchanges with Holland blossomed in rapid progress and subsequently inspired Japan to trade with the rest of the world. In so doing, they helped bring about what is now known as the Meiji Restoration.

All these years later, in this corner of Nagasaki Prefecture, Japan has turned to Holland to help it understand just how environmental preservation and large-scale development can walk hand in hand. And that Dejima Island trading house is yet another of the actual buildings that have found their way into Japan's vision of a new Dutch town. It will feature visual presentations that document the long history of Japan-Holland relations. And among the resort's 12 museums is the Siebold Museum, named after Philipp Franz von Siebold, a physician, who first arrived in Japan as medical officer to the trading house. When he returned to Leiden, Holland, Siebold took with him many documents and artifacts that documented Japanese life in the late Edo and early Meiji periods. These later became known as the Siebold Collection.

Many of the items, including drawings, etchings, and town bylaws are now on show at the Siebold Museum, and they speak more articulately than anything of what resort officials call "the 400-year Holland-Japan exchange."

I spent much of my two days in Huis Ten Bosch trying to find the exact words to define it — not its beauty, this time, but its function, its reason for being, its purpose. Finally, while walking leisurely with my translator before an exorbitant buffet dinner attended by almost 1,000 staffers and guests, I decided that it was a resort, yes, but something of a Japanese architectural showcase, too. After all, it probably sports the best condominiums, houses, hotels, shops, restaurants, and marinas anywhere in Japan. That night, however, while strolling alone this time, I decided that it was something even more than both of these.

First, it represented the Japanese flair for copying, for imitating anything that may satisfy a dream. In this was manifested its will to capture foreign settings — to internationalize, to show goodwill, to build cultural bridges with a world it has tried so hard to be a part of.

It is also a showcase for Japanese engineering — as witnessed by the elegant yet sturdy buildings and bridges, as well as a plant that sucks in sea water and converts it to drinking water at the rate of 1,000 metric tons a day — not to mention its obsession with meticulous detail. Even the roadside garbage receptacles have brass fittings, and the boats, buses, and taxi cabs — all with Nissan engines — have been made to resemble vehicles of a bygone era.

Finally, Huis Ten Bosch represents the innate way the Japanese provide facilities that will ultimately appeal — naturally — to their yearning and taste for things of the very highest quality. More than even this, however, it is a place the Japanese hope may eventually become a world playground, where tycoons from Taipei, perhaps, Hong Kong, Singapore, Shanghai or Seoul can retreat from the bustle of a corporate world to seal their business deals. Says Paul Takada: "We want Huis Ten Bosch to become an international resort — a base for international conferences and cultural events on an international scale. After all, its location makes it a convenient gateway to Japan from many other parts of Asia."

Early on my second day at Huis Ten Bosch, I rose in

my room at the Hotel Europe — an exact copy of its namesake, a bastion of dignity that sits like a splendidly ornate block of granite in the center of Amsterdam — to eat breakfast in one of the two main dining rooms. While being afforded the opportunity to explore a unique place, I was also being pampered.

Huis Ten Bosch is not without faults, however, and most of these stem from Japanese input where it is completely unnecessary. No one, of course, can object to the Japanese staff of some 2,000 people who do everything from drive the taxis cabs and buses, and work in the hotels, to serve in virtually all of the shops and maintain the buildings. Nor can anyone pick fault with the cross-cultural charm of seeing Japanese workers dressed in traditional Dutch garb tending the nearly 500,000 tulips that stand like sentinels reaching for the sun. What is wrong with Huis Ten Bosch has more to do with intruding on what it sets out to be — a corner of old Holland with a series of rather inane attractions that, quite frankly, detract from the theme.

The few museums are scant, indeed, and the Disney-like attractions — a ride into space, for instance, and some animated film shows — seem to me to be aimed at a 13-year-old mentality while having little, or nothing, to do with Holland at all.

There is also the matter of a name — Huis Ten Bosch — that can only be properly read or pronounced by a Dutch person, and distance: that long bus ride from Nagasaki Airport, and an even longer one to Fukuoka Airport. Added to this, the on-site expense for ordinary people for almost everything — my room at Hotel Europe costs ¥30,000 a night, for instance — cannot be dismissed. But then, perhaps the so-called ordinary folk are not what the Nagasaki Holland Village Company Inc. is trying to attract.

As Huis Ten Bosch begins its life away from the bustle of big-time Japan, it must attract four million people each year if it is to begin to wipe out the huge investment so far incurred. In it's favor is its location, suitably situated to garner customers from such east Asian centers as Beijing, Shanghai, Taipei, Hong Kong, and Manila, all of them less than four hours away by air. High speed boats are also planned, and JR Kyushu is already at work, laying a track that will take visitors directly into the ornate, pink-bricked, gray-roofed Huis Ten Bosch Station, which must be one of the best looking rail terminals in the world.

The new line will eventually ensure that the trip from Nagasaki can be accomplished in one hour and 10 minutes, and the one from Fukuoka in one hour and 25 minutes. So all is not lost.

The biggest boost to the resort town, however, will be its incredible in-house service. Between more long walks, I sat in Hotel Europe's huge, gleaming wood-floor lobby and marveled at how the staffers went about their business with a fastidiousness and sense of hospitality that may well be unprecedented in our time. The only doors most guests will ever open for themselves there will doubtless be the door to their rooms.

This is Huis Ten Bosch, rich, refined, elegant.

As I joined the convoy of buses loaded with journalist to travel to Fukuoka Airport this time, for the early evening flight back to Tokyo, I was still slightly overwhelmed with what I had seen.

"Is Japan ready for it," I began to ask myself. "Is the rest of Asia ready for it? Is the world?"

Only time — and money to promote Huis Ten Bosch — will tell.

The day I kissed the dentist

April 18, 1992

I HAVE DECIDED THAT I like Japanese dentists and miss them when I don't have to see them. That may sound odd, but it is nonetheless true. Just as a customer in a shop is revered as a kind of god in Japan, so is a patient. Japanese dentists don't sing or chant when their patients walk in holding their jaws, but they are very pleased to see them. I discovered this about a year ago when, while munching on a nut-filled chocolate bar, I broke a back tooth. On the recommendation of my friend, the Roman Catholic priest in Shin-Okubo, I trundled off to see a woman who practiced near Tamachi Station.

Whereas North American dentists *tell* you what they are about to do to you, Japanese dentists ask for your permission first.

My best friend, Hershel Bernstein, is reputed to be one of Canada's most eminent dentists, having pioneered all manner of surgical techniques to help people who have no teeth at all. He is so deft at installing steel posts into jawbones so he can eventually hook dentures onto them that the simple chore of filling a minuscule cavity no longer seems to challenge him. It is reflected in his voice.

Once I am captive in his chair, he ceases to be my friend.

"Keep still and open big," he growls. "C'mon, open big!"

He then freezes my entire head and begins to make that little hole bigger. Finally, having packed it with cement, he presents me with a bill for $100! By this time, my mouth is so lifeless I am unable to argue.

My first Japanese dentist, a friendly, middle-aged woman, wasn't like that at all. She invited me to place my *meishi* and proof of my medical insurance on a green plastic tray, then, having fitted me with a pale blue bib, proceeded to poke around inside my mouth, whining with compassion.

"May I cap that broken tooth?" she asked softly. "But first, may I clean out all the decay?"

Standing beside me with her big hypodermic needle, her eyes above her white mask were huge pools of compassion. "Is it all right to shoot you?" she inquired.

I gripped the arms of the chair anticipating an injection I never even felt.

Later, when that same dentist decided to cap another tooth, her dark eyes melted once more as she prepared to give me another anesthetic. "May I shot you?" she said this time.

Once shot and fixed up, I was ceremoniously given a bill for ¥700.

Anyway, all that isn't nearly as important as what happened when I returned to Canada last March, and Dr. Hershel Bernstein examined my new dental work. He knows, as I do, that there are a lot of mouths in Japan like chain saws. So he viewed mine with suspicion.

"Hmmmm," he said eventually. "Those crowns fit very well. I am very impressed."

Unfortunately, however, the woman who installed them has moved, and because I can't read the Tokyo phone book I have been unable to find her.

Not to worry. Shortly after coming back to Japan last June, I met another dentist — a young woman named Kaori Okazaki who also practices in Tamachi. "May I shoot you?" she asked, then capped a third tooth. According to the terms of my medical insurance, she charged me ¥570.

Then came problems with a fourth tooth — a tenacious abscess. What Kaori Okazaki did was this: She removed the crown, with a sledgehammer, I think, burned out the nerves from each of the tooth's three roots, then drilled a canal to the apex of one of these, hoping that the abscess would drain through it.

Nothing went according to plan. After six bouts of antibiotics, and almost as many appointments that put us on a first-name basis, I had a swelling on the outer side of my gum the size of a sparrow's egg. So the day came when, to her utter regret, Kaori would have to incise it. The night before, of course, I woke up contemplating the worst. When the time came for her to do it, I told myself, she would chicken out because cutting someone's gum is not a pleasant thing to have to do. I also recall telling myself I did not have an abscess at all. It was a cyst, and a malignant one into the bargain!

The following morning, however, Kaori was optimistic. "May I give you a shot?" she asked this time.

"Yes," I said. "Of scotch."

She'd seen me so many times that her English had improved, if nothing else.

She laughed a little, then plunged her hypodermic needle so far into my upper gum I thought it would soon appear through my left ear. It didn't, though, and I am now so happy to tell you that I have survived this ordeal. My tooth has been recapped, and my gum is like new. I am misery-free and lucky.

Lucky? Yes. I had found another Japanese dentist who could be ranked with any general dentist I have met anywhere. "Your abscess has gone," Kaori Okazaki announced, her big eyes shining with pride. "Maybe it will not come back."

I was so relieved, that I did something naughty, particularly in Japan where emotions are kept under lock and key. I sprang from the chair, and, with lips still numb from an anesthetic that was fast paralyzing my brain, kissed the dentist's forehead.

As I guiltily paid her a mere ¥640 for her fine and exacting work, Kaori Okazaki removed her surgical mask. "I'm very, very sorry your treatment has ended," she said. "I will miss seeing you."

God, I like Japanese dentists.

Mami's story

April 25, 1992

SOMETIMES, WHEN A WOMAN is dying, she directs that her body may be taken by the doctors and sliced into pieces so that medical science may benefit from what is found therein. In much the same way, Mami does that now, though for the moment she is still alive. Her story, which begins three years ago when she and six other Filipino women arrived at Japan's Narita Airport to become sex slaves, is not one she likes to tell. She does it anyway, in the ardent hope that mankind may be the richer, and that the Japanese government might do something to help thousands of women like her.

Mami is not her real name, of course. That was given to her in Manila by a Japanese man who recruited her to go to Tokyo as an entertainer. The fact that she could neither dance nor sing when the offer was made did not arouse her suspicion. She was too young, after all — just 15, and the oldest in a family of eleven children, all of whom had been born in Tagum on Mindanao Island. It was there that her father built his farm, from which the Philippines National Army forced the family to leave.

To protect themselves from the New People's Army, Mami, her parents and brothers and sisters carted everything they owned to a camp four kilometers away. There, the captain of the local army squadron recognized Mami's need to help her family financially and introduced

194

her to the recruiter who told her that if she learned to perform by singing in a karaoke bar on Manila's Mabini Street, he would get her a fake passport that bore a visa that would enable her to work in Japan as an entertainer.

"He said I would be hired as a singer and a dancer at a famous Tokyo hotel," Mami recalls. Nothing was farther from the truth.

When she and her six friends arrived at Narita, they were met by a man who confiscated their passports and took them to an office in Shinjuku. There, in daily sessions, they were taught how to strip. Says Mami, "I objected and said I'd been trained in Manila as a singer, but no one listened to me."

Well, that's not quite right. The boss and his partner did listen, but shook their heads. They said that all women hired abroad had to start working immediately to pay back the money the company had so far invested to bring them here. Since singing was precarious, they would have to be strippers.

Foreign women, mostly from Taiwan, Thailand, and the Philippines, first began working in Japan's sex entertainment industry in the early 1980s. Today, despite new laws passed in June 1990 to curb the number of unskilled or unwanted foreign workers in Japan in general, the plight of women like Mami is no better. According to the Tokyo-based Asian Women's Association, there are as many as 80,000 of them, all working in the booming sex industry as prisoners of economic necessity, and of organized crime.

Mami's first job was in a basement bar in Shinjuku's Kabuki-cho district, from where she was taken to nearly every large center in Japan. She appeared in clubs and strip halls, staying in each place for about 10 days before being whisked away in the night under the pretense that the police were getting suspicious. "Sometimes," she says, "because I couldn't speak or read Japanese, I didn't know what was going on or where I was."

After three months, her escort told her that all she really had in her passport was a tourist visa, and that her only hope of making money to send to her family was by working illegally. In a snack bar in Nagoya, a yakuza boss announced that her debt to the company was still ¥600,000, and that she would have to hand over all the money she earned until it was paid while working as a prostitute. When Mami refused, she was dragged screaming into a small room behind the kitchen, and beaten.

From then on, customers asked her, "How much?"

"I am not an object for sale," Mami replied. She remembers, "If the owner had heard me say that, he would have increased my debt and punched me in the face like he often did when things didn't go his way."

Long after she had calculated that the money she owed had been paid, she still did not see any of her earnings. That's when she and two other women sex slaves decided to escape. Mami contacted some Filipino friends and rested in their apartment for six days over the New Year holiday before finding work as a waitress on the outskirts of Nagoya. "I'd picked up quite a bit of Japanese by then," she reflects. "At least, it was enough to get by on."

A month later, and to her horror, the yakuza discovered where she was. A man she had never seen before waylaid her as she left work one night, wrestled her into a car, and took her back to the snack bar where she was beaten about the head so much that she was unable to open her eyes. She was then locked in a house for several days, and, as soon as her wounds had healed, was delivered to the streets again under the deep scrutiny of a pimp.

"There were times when I was afraid for my life," Mami recalls. "There were also times when I felt I should go to the police and give myself up."

In this, there was one problem. She had heard, she says, that in smaller cities the length and breadth of Japan, the police prefer not to bother themselves with runaway prostitutes who also happen to be illegal workers. Rather than arrest them and hand them over to immigration authorities, they find it easier to simply return them to the men from whom they have fled.

For all this, and despite continuing to work another six weeks for no money, Mami planned another escape, this time with a young Filipino prostitute who had been sharing a room with her in a house opposite the snack bar. It was Mami's idea to hand a note to a mutual customer, asking him to tell the police that they needed help.

The plan may have misfired because three days later, while both women were working elsewhere, two men arrived at the snack bar asking for them by name. Mami still does not know whether or not they were detectives planning to return later. "What if they weren't cops?" she asks. "I get weak when I think of what might have happened to us."

Instead of waiting, she and her friend hurriedly jammed their belongings into two plastic bags and escaped. Later, after spending two nights in a vacant warehouse on the edge of town, they gave themselves up. "The police must have seen the terror on our faces," Mami recalls, "because they were actually quite kind to us."

A week after that, she and her friend were deported, and there the story should have a logical ending. But it doesn't. Back in Manila, Mami returned to the sordid world of Filipino and Japanese recruiters, promoters, agents, managers, traders, club owners, yakuza men, and gangs, "all the elements that sort of make up the multi-billion-dollar sex industry that stretches right across Asia," she says.

She did it this time mostly as a singer in a strip-cum-karaoke club on Mabini Street, though she admits to returning briefly to prostitution in the busy city of Olongapo. "That," she recalls, "was until I decided I couldn't compete with 16,000 other prostitutes there."

It was also until she felt unusually tired and consulted a doctor. Somewhere along the way — who knows where, exactly — she had contracted AIDS. "Being an HIV carrier," Mami wrote recently to the Asia Women's Association, which followed her case, "sort of settles my future, wouldn't you say? And for that, I will never forget Japan, or the man who sent me there. All too often women are blamed for being prostitutes. I really had no choice in the matter, and I have paid very, very dearly."

The arrow must be straight

May 2, 1992

AS A SMALL BOY GROWING UP in England, I envisioned myself as the great hunter. On Saturdays, friends and I would each take a bow and arrow into a field and try to fell rabbits. That we missed all the time was testament to the crudeness of our equipment, usually made from little trees, and our impetuousness, made of youth. My arrow, I can tell you, always seemed to career off recklessly, and I had soon earned the reputation of being the only kid on the street who could somehow shoot an arrow sideways.

What I was doing wrong never really sunk in until a few weeks ago when my friend Gikon invited me to watch him perform Japanese archery in Yokohama. He and his 120-odd co-members of a club there can fire a single arrow 28 meters to pierce the middle of a target only 36 cm in diameter. Sometimes, they actually hit the bull's eye, which is set 28 cm from the ground.

The feat calls for both meditation and concentration during the long, ritualistic ceremony that precedes the actual taking up of a position. From then on, the noble act of raising the center of the big bow high above the head, and then lowering it carefully until the arrow is at eye level, is pure, graceful ballet at its best.

This comprises art, style, athletic prowess, and, oh, yes, skill in knowing how to hold and release the arrow when the bowstring is drawn back almost as hard as you can pull it. The rest, according to Japanese belief, is entirely up to the arrow, which, once in flight, is said to have a life of its very own.

To listen to Gikon, it doesn't really matter if it hits the target or not. There is a certain satisfaction in simply releasing the arrow and watching it take its path. If, however, all the preparation has been done properly and this can take many years to perfect, chances are it will. Certainly, it will not slap the big wall sideways and harmlessly.

The analogy is not hard to find. Archery seems to embrace two main elements: stylish performance and meticulous preparation. The deep, contemplative concentration needed to accomplish it properly can be likened to the deep, contemplative element needed to conduct big business, for which the Japanese have become legendary. No matter how large or small, Japanese companies are generally successful because, as in the case of archery, they have prepared well to penetrate the marketplace. And when this homework — research, analysis, and product quality — is left only partially done, things can go tragically awry.

Especially in today's competitive world.

Halfway through the afternoon, Gikon took me onto a small range at the rear of the building, presumably where I could do no harm, handed me a bow and a couple of arrows, and, after a quick lesson in archery, invited me to try to hit a bale of straw from only three meters. The inevitable occurred. My arrow had a short, unfocused, purposeless life, for I missed the straw and watched it sail off far to the left, and slap itself harmlessly, and sideways, against a hedge.

Back on the range, Gikon took up his elegant position once more, and, as if to show my ineptness, hit the bull's eye at his very next attempt.

I THOUGHT YOU MIGHT enjoy David Simons' little piece, spotted in a publication called *E.T.C, English Teachers' Connection,* released recently by the Yokohama YMCA. Simons, himself a teacher, lists those things that remind foreigners they are now very much a part of Japan.

You have been in Japan a long time, he says, when you:

- Start bowing while speaking on the telephone
- Don't take the waiter or the waitress outside the restaurant to point out your order in the window
- Stop responding to cries of "Welcome!" and "Thank you!" from the staff in restaurants or department stores
- Stop giving up your seat on trains
- Stop counting your change
- Know when and how to pay on buses
- Don't even try to buy a pair of shoes in your size, because there probably isn't one
- Realize that when you break a ¥10,000 note you can kiss it goodbye

"Any additional contributions would be welcome," David Simons says. So I thought I'd give him a list compiled by my wife.

She feels you can consider yourself a part of Japan when:

- You start bowing to your spouse

- You are completely unafraid to doze on the trains in case you miss your station or someone steals your wallet. (My wife sleeps everywhere. She has even been known to make her bed on the ironing board.)
- You stop smiling at other foreigners on the street. (Most of the foreigners I see aren't smiling.)
- You replace "hello" with "*moushi-moushi*"
- You leave your briefcase on a restaurant table while using the toilet — without worrying if someone will steal it. (I take my briefcase with me.)
- You stop eating on the trains and the streets. (I do both — shamelessly.)

NOT TOO LONG AGO, I left a chicken pie on the Chuo Line, but, despite ardent efforts, never got it back. It was probably among the 1.48 million lost items that ended up in the custody of the National Police Agency last year. Predictably, most of these were umbrellas — 370,000 of them, and that, says an agency report, means that an average 3,000 umbrellas were lost on each rainy day. Only one in 74 were retrieved by their rightful owners.

Other items handed in to the police included all manner of wallets that contained bank cards, credit cards, and identification cards, and only half of them were claimed — like the handbags and watches turned in.

"Some of these," says the Police Agency, "were fakes anyway."

Interestingly, the amount of lost money claimed — ¥3.4 billion — was more than three times that reported lost. This means, of course, that a lot of people kept what they found.

Nonetheless, ¥2.6 billion was returned to rightful owners and ¥650 million that was unclaimed was given to those people who had been honest enough to hand it in. What cash left over was sent to the Tokyo Metropolitan Government to spend on public works projects.

There was still no word, however, on my chicken pie.

Japan's forgotten boys

May 2, 1992

IT WAS, IN ITS WAY, a stroke of genius that has an all-too-familiar echo. Back through time, composers and librettists have always sought out patrons, and the biggest of these was the Church, which financed and inspired men like Bach, Handel, and Haydn. And things are no different today, as witnessed by the flash of inspiration displayed by an outspoken, black-bearded Japanese opera bass-baritone named Eduardo Ishita.

There has been nothing special about Eduardo's career, except that instead of trying to find a place on the international opera circuit when he graduated from a Tokyo music college, he decided to do what he could on home turf. He and a few friends founded their own company — the 16-year-old Tokyo Opera Association, one of several such groups that takes grand opera around Japan.

About four years ago, a group of people in Omura City, Nagasaki Prefecture, not far from Hasami, where Eduardo lives with his wife Kayoko (a soprano he met in college) and their five sons, asked him to write the libretto of an opera. All members of local historical societies, those people wanted to celebrate the 400th anniversary of an important event in an important period of Japanese history. They wanted Eduardo to document the lives of four young boys, all of them

Roman Catholics, and all from that part of Japan, who were said to have been at the forefront of the country's first cultural communication with the West, and who suffered needlessly for it.

Chosen as the deputies of Christian feudal lords, the boys, then aged only 14, were sent to Europe from Nagasaki to meet Pope Gregory XIII of Rome and King Phillip II of Spain, as well as Christians in other nations. Their journey was known as the "Tensho Mission" because it took place during the Tensho Era (1573-1592). Eight years later, when the boys returned to Japan as young men — to continue their work with a special knowledge of European culture, technology, and Biblical teaching — they discovered that Shogun Hideyoshi had taken it upon himself to outlaw Christianity. Their struggle was only just beginning.

It ended somewhat sadly, which is just fine for opera. Michael Chijiwa became discouraged about the prospect of Christianity taking root in Japan and renounced his faith, Mancio Ito died of exhaustion while trying to win converts, Martino Hara met a lonely death in exile on the island of Macau, and Julian Nakaura overcame the ban on Christianity and died an intellectual martyr.

It was a story that immediately fired Eduardo's imagination. "Even today," he says, "you can wonder if Japan treats its minorities as well as it should." And, a year or so later, when his libretto was finally complete, he handed it to composer Minao Shibata, who had agreed to set it to music. Fittingly, Ishita called his work *The Forgotten Boys*.

But that was not all. To ensure that it got the recognition he felt it deserved, he decided to seek the help of...guess what? Right! Perhaps the longest-serving and most devout patron of all the arts — the Roman Catholic Church.

"I would like the Pope to see and enjoy this," Ishita said. "After all, it is about four young Catholics, and how they tried so hard to spread their faith."

Just how far he could spread the knowledge of his work at the Vatican, however, remained to be seen. But Eduardo Ishita is a patient, determined man, who, like most people who follow careers in musical theater, grow to become impervious to disappointment.

He was born in Osaka in 1947, the second son of a Japanese father, a retired businessman, and a Filipino mother who spends her time helping foreign people — many from the Philippines — who experience difficulties when they come to Japan to work. "There is a lot of tragedy in a lot of young lives in Japan," Eduardo says ruefully.

His first introduction to music came when he was enthralled by a Beethoven string quartet he heard as a student at Osaka's Kozu High School. "Beethoven's music," he reflects, "is for people who want to be elevated, Bach's is for people who need help from God, and Mozart's is for people who want to enjoy life."

Eduardo enjoyed life from the moment he thought he might like to be a musician himself, and studied singing. At 26, he was good enough to sing roles in such Mozartian operatic masterpieces as *Cosi fan tutte*, *Don Giovanni*, *The Magic Flute*, and *The Marriage of Figaro*. Nothing delighted him more, however, than when *The Forgotten Boys* was readying itself for opening night.

After its debut performance in Nagasaki in August

1990, Eduardo decided the opera should travel throughout Japan — and then the world. So, that October, he sent the libretto, as well as a video, to a man named Peter Junichi Iwahashi, secretary general of the Catholic Bishops' Conference of Japan. His request: "I would like the Pope to know my opera." Iwahashi, in turn, took it upon himself to send the package to Archbishop William A. Carew, the Apostolic Pro-Nuncio in Tokyo.

"I presume that your Excellency is busy as usual, especially in the last season of the liturgical calendar," Iwahashi wrote. Then he introduced Eduardo the opera baritone, and his new work. "He desires to present the opera to His Holiness to close his journey of performances," he said, and gave more details of the plot.

Iwahashi called the opera "wonderful and meaningful" and added (as if it should really have mattered): "Mr. Eduardo Ishita is the second son of a Japanese father and a Filipino mother. All members of the family, with the singular exception of Eduardo, are baptized in the Catholic Church."

Says Eduardo, "Actually, when it comes to religion, I'm nothing. Just an opera singer. But I do believe in God."

Another letter to William Carew was sent by Takashi Matsumoto, Omura City's mayor. He called Eduardo's opera "a wonderful gift" and "a masterpiece," and said, "I think this is a time for Japan to contribute widely to the welfare of the world instead of being content with the status quo. I became keenly aware of the import-ance of learning from history, when the present policy and state of the world is questioned by the world."

Meanwhile, Eduardo waited. He met regularly with his four colleagues at the opera association to plan an international version of the opera and lamented that although *The Forgotten Boys* had been a resounding success, opera in Japan is not as popular as he would like it to be. "Classical music," he says, "somehow lifts Man up and makes him more human. Many of the Japanese don't want to be lifted up."

Maybe not, but they are certainly tolerant, particularly with the noise in the neighborhood as the agile voices of big basses, burly baritones, lusty tenors, buxom sopranos, and tenacious contraltos spill into the night. Fortunately, the little building that houses the opera association abuts a shoe polishing factory on one side, so no one cares too much about noise there. But on the other side, and upstairs, there is a cluster of rundown apartments. "But the people love us and know what we are trying to do," says Ishita. "They know we are trying to put operas together. They understand that wherever there is opera, music must be made."

One afternoon in December 1990, while he and the opera company were rehearsing in Izu, south of Tokyo, the phone rang. It was Carew's secretary. The Pope not only liked both the libretto and the video of *The Forgotten Boys*, but wanted to meet Eduardo Ishita.

"Of course, I was quite happy," Eduardo reflects with typical Japanese reserve.

To show it, he picked up the telephone and called a friend, Takashi Ishii, who lives in Cremona, Italy, where he makes violins similar to those played by those four boys back in the 16th century. "You're coming to meet the Pope with me," Eduardo said.

He also called his wife and his mother and took both of them when he went to the Vatican on April 10, 1991.

"I like your opera very much," the Pope said, and agreed to receive Eduardo again the following week.

Now Eduardo Ishita is planning to recast his opera and take it overseas, principally to Macau, Lisbon, and Rome — among the places the four boys visited when they left Japan.

But how will the Pope help him?

"Well," says Eduardo Ishita, "he blessed me and my opera and wished me success. That's enough, isn't it?"

One man's gomi....

May 16, 1992

"COME QUICKLY!" said my wife Irene, rushing into the apartment breathlessly. "There's something you've got to see — on the *gomi*. Go down and get it before it disappears!"

"The gomi?" I asked.

"Yes, the garbage — downstairs!"

I love gomi. I always have. Not ours, though. The people where we live only seem to throw away baby carriages and futon, and rarely anything worthwhile. Today, however, was an exception, and I have to congratulate Irene for recognizing it. I got dressed and, on her advice, went down before the truck arrived to haul the mess away.

There, standing sedately on the floor by the entrance to the cavernous place where the gomi lives with a couple of neighborhood cats, was a television set. We already have one set, so why would we want another? The answer, I think, is quite simple. Two are better than one. And anyway, there's always something very pleasant about getting something for nothing. Simple Western psychology, right?

I wheeled the television set up to the apartment on a luggage trolley for, I presumed, major repairs. Not only do I like the gomi, I also enjoy fixing things. There's a certain satisfaction in that as well. When I lived in a foreigners' house in Iogi, I found a broken bookcase on the gomi, mended it, and I used it for the

18 months I was there. It was the best bookcase I have ever owned.

Our room came furnished, but a furnished room in Japan is one equipped with a chair and a coffee table. That, and extraordinarily high prices in Japan, is why a lot of other foreigners like the gomi, too. I have heard of people furnishing their entire apartments with gomi cast-offs. And in Japan, they will tell you, items retrieved from the gomi are of an unusually high quality.

In the first place, the Japanese like good things. In the second, they seem to tire of them quickly. In the third, they do not have the space to hoard. So they simply throw unwanted articles away, long before their time. I mean, who in their right mind would discard a good-looking Sony? Or a solid, rosewood bookcase? Can't the Japanese buy a few tools and fix things like other people do?

The landlord at that foreigners' house, a pleasant, free-smiling man named Yoshikazu Yaji, barred anything found on the gomi from his premises. Not only was it likely to be dirty, he maintained, but even after it had been scrubbed there remained a strong likelihood of it being contaminated — "with bad spirits." Apart from being affable and genteel, Mr. Yaji was also incorrigibly superstitious, like a lot of other Japanese people I know. "The gomi is bad," he'd often say, shaking his head while humming and sucking in air. "It is very bad."

Well, with recommendations like that, it was not surprising that it should yield quite a lot of useful things for quite a few of his tenants. One young woman, a bar singer, found a stereo system on the gomi. It looked wonderful, but didn't work. Another, a teacher, retrieved a chair, and yet another a picture that she hung proudly over her futon. The best gomi story of all, however, concerned my friend Gary. He and his wife Patty had been in the foreigners' house a mere two weeks when they decided they couldn't stand the communal kitchen, let alone some of the silly conversations that went on around them night after night — and I can't say that I ever blamed them — and were already arranging to move into an unfurnished apartment just along the road. They now wanted as many useful things they could lay their hands on, especially if they were free. That's when Gary stalked Iogi specifically to examine gomi. It was February and cold, but he did it anyway.

One afternoon, he spotted an electric oven at the roadside. Actually, now I come to think of it, it was a microwave oven and broiler all rolled into one — a big, bulky piece of kitchenware if ever there was one, and quite a rare find in Japan. Most Japanese seem to spend their entire lives cooking morsels of meat and fish in toasters.

Although this oven was incredibly dirty, Gary and Patty were unperturbed. Gary simply borrowed my bicycle and rushed out to buy a selection of spray-on cleaning liquids and pads, and, after spending four hours scraping away the grease and grime with a knife, he and Patty were ready to polish. Soon there emerged, on a sheet of newspaper strewn across their nine-tatami room, a magnificent, handsome, chrome-plated contraption that was fit to cook meals for an emperor. It had never looked so clean since the day it was bought, I reckon.

Now Gary and Patty were set. Or so they thought.

That was until around eight that night — when the police arrived. What Gary thought was on the gomi had, in fact, been deposited temporarily at the curbside by the couple that was moving out of a house. Someone had seen a blond, blue-eyed foreigner heaving the contraption onto his shoulder and walking away with it. It was not too difficult for the local police to track down exactly where that foreigner lived.

Had Gary known the oven had not been discarded, of course, he would not have taken it. And, with Mr. Yaji's help as both a translator and mediator the police believed him. In fact, while Gary sat in a pool of remorse, wondering if he would be deported this week or next, the cops had quite a good laugh about his plight. They were pretty understanding, modern-day cops, if you ask me. The oven's owners, however — a couple with three children — didn't see the funny side at all. At first, the husband apparently did. But when he detected his wife's anger, because the moving company's truck had to depart Iogi without her prized oven, leaving her with nothing to cook in, he changed. His wife wanted her oven back, immediately, and said it had to be delivered to their new home — in Yokohama!

That's where I came in. I contacted various delivery services, but they refused to cart the oven because it was too heavy. A friend thought he might be able to deliver it in his car that weekend, but changed his mind. And a moving company said it would be very happy to take the oven to Yokohama, for ¥25,000 — sometime in June!

I forget now how Gary actually reunited the woman

with her oven. I seem to recall that with more of Mr. Yaji's help, he hired a smaller, less expensive delivery service that charged him only ¥4,000, and the woman received her oven two days later. At any rate, this brush with the gomi — and the police — ended up costing him more than he bargained for. What annoyed him most of all, I think, was that the woman never even telephoned to thank him and his wife for scrubbing the oven clean.

My television set has probably never been cleaner since the day it was bought, either, by the way. I washed it thoroughly, affixed some aerial wire, plugged it in, then, without having to do any repairs at all, viewed a perfect picture! Mind you, I didn't much like what I was watching — some stupid show about a man who cures gallstones by putting his hands on people's foreheads (a funny place to have gallstones, I thought), and a succession of home videos that showed young children hurting themselves — but I have to admit that it is the best television set I have ever owned. I think Gary and Patty would be very proud of me, even a little envious, perhaps.

The latest, though, is this: Gary and Patty, having settled permanently in Japan, and are cooking morsels of meat and fish in a toaster, and I have since decided that I don't much like having an extra television set. The programs aired in Tokyo don't even warrant one, let alone two. So I want to donate my find, evil spirits and all, to a worthy cause. If I don't — or if I can't — I may have to do something uncharacteristically sacrilegious for a Mr. Fix It-cum-hoarder like me. I may have to put it back where I found it. On the gomi.

Obscenity? Or stupidity?

May 23, 1992

I WAS REMINDED this week of a friend, the well-known Canadian broadcaster Clyde Gilmour, who used to tell a story about his days as a Canadian Forces public relations officer. One day, the inevitable occurred. A haphazard typist posted his name and profession on a bulletin board and omitted the "l" from "public." There and then, poor Clyde became a "pubic" relations officer, and, since he was assigned to the Royal Canadian Navy, was not able to live it down until he returned to civilian life after World War II.

What made me think of Clyde was a letter I came upon here in Tokyo when I did my weekly search of the English-language media. I do this primarily to look for readers' letters, particularly those that tell us what irks readers most. At one point, I contemplated assigning a translator to read what Japanese readers were saying in the Japanese-language print media, but she advised me against it.

"Japanese newspapers and magazines," she said, "usually only print letters that are complimentary and aren't controversial. And besides, Japanese people are not very good at expressing their opinions. They are kind of frightened to, if you get what I mean."

I do, of course, and this explains why this country still has a lot of work to do if it is to become truly inter-national.

Anyway, I thought you would enjoy a letter written by a man named Brian Clacey, who lives in Kitami, Hokkaido. In part, it is about the ludicrousness of Japan's obscenity laws, or — if you consider the awful trash that seeps into the comic strips and, believe it or not, into the mass-circulation sports newspapers — the acute lack of them. Or maybe his letter is about double standards, hypocrisy, or plain stupidity.

It reminded me so much of Clyde Gilmour because, while he became a "pubic" relations officer by error, there are Japanese civil servants who have become "pubic" relations officers by appointment. They seem to spend their days scanning magazines for pubic hair. Brian Clacey, whose letter appeared in *The Daily Yomiuri* where the editors sure took a bold step in deciding to print it, dealt with the issue this way:

I found a report (May 2 or 3) of the police giving an obscenity warning to the Shukan Post *because of the photographs that appeared in an issue of this magazine. Pubic hair was visible in some of them! This report is almost surreal in its bizarreness.*

In a country being slowly buried in its own rubbish and strangled by its own pollution, and where political corruption and vote-buying is so rife that it makes the word "democracy" farcical, in a society that pounds its young into a state of blank-eyed apathy, and has an "education" system that teaches them how not to think, in a nation that has achieved "internationalization" to the point of being reviled internationally as the home of self-centered "economic animals" and eco-outlaws who preside over the rape and despoliation of the countries in which they invest — in a country such as this, one would think that the powers that be would be spoiled for choices when it came to selecting problems to address.

What, however, do they take decisive action over? Pubic hair!

Truly, the Land of the Rising Sun becomes more the Land of Cloud Cuckoo every day.

These are my sentiments exactly, sir. The sad point is that if it were not for the foreign community's letter writers, and, dare I say, some of Japan's more adventurous foreign columnists, such paradoxes would never be pointed out. Meanwhile, I challenge the English-language Japanese newspapers to write editorials with the tone of that letter, pointing up some of the ironies it contains. I bet they won't, though. There would, I think, be an awful lot of pubic hair covering the *wa* (the group harmony), so to speak — in public.

I THOUGHT YOU MIGHT enjoy some anecdotes that help put some elements of Japan into true focus. They speak for themselves, I think.

On Saturday, I took my wife and daughter to McDonald's for breakfast, and while there, did what most foreigners in Japan have to do. I pointed at what each of us wanted to eat — a picture of a set meal that included an egg McMuffin, a portion of fried potatoes, and a cup of coffee. I don't know what it cost, but it was surely less expensive than it would have been had I ordered each item separately.

The woman who served me said that the breakfast set for that day was no longer being served. Why?

Because it was only available until 10 a.m., and was then immediately discontinued.

The time on the clock as our order was rejected? *One minute past ten*!

I'll repeat that for you because you might find this principle of sticking to the rules absolutely, and without bending them, as ridiculous as I do. It was 10:01 a.m. And if the truth was known, I had walked into the shop about five minutes earlier.

Quite obviously, the woman couldn't make a decision herself, so she called another woman. They held a quick meeting until one of them went away and returned with the manager. I explained how silly and unfair it was that I should not be able to buy the breakfast set at 10:01 a.m., especially since I had been waiting in line for it for some minutes. He agreed.

The moral of the story, I think, is fight for what you think is right.

NOT LONG BEFORE, I had bought some batteries in a small shop at Tamachi Station. The bill came to ¥178. All the change in my pocket amounted to ¥177, and I offered it gladly. As you will understand, I was merely trying to be helpful. The clerk didn't seem to understand this, though, and shook his head.

"No," he said, and pointed to the amount shown on the cash register — ¥178.

For a moment, I thought of leaving the shop and plucking ¥1 from the sidewalk. I remembered that in the mornings, the steps at Tamachi Station are fairly littered with ¥1 coins!

I finally decided to hand the clerk a ¥10,000 note, and from this he took the money for the batteries — gladly.

Ironically, in Shinjuku, a week or so ago, I bought some chocolate with a ¥1,000 note. My change should have included ¥2, but the woman who served me said, apologetically, of course, "I'm so terribly sorry, and I hope you will excuse me for it, but I haven't any one-yen coins!" She appeared beside herself with grief.

"Don't worry about it," I told her. "A couple of yen won't break me."

I THINK I HAVE already told you that I collect CDs that can be bought for ¥1,000, mostly at JR stations. Occasionally I will spend ¥1,500 on a CD, but this is not usually necessary. Many of the most magnificent phonographic performances of the past 30 years or so are now available for less, and it is these that I want to collect.

When I enter a record store, it is hard for me to explain all of this. And anyway, most of the clerks have never even heard of Bach, Mozart, Beethoven, and Brahms, let alone listened to their music. So I usually ask, "Do you have any one-thousand-yen CDs?"

I did this in Yokohama the other day and carefully wrote the amount I wanted to spend on a piece of paper. The clerk shook his head. I looked around the store anyway, and found quite a large collection of CDs — for ¥970 each! They were just what I wanted, and I told the clerk so. He shrugged.

My daughter, who was with me, and who speaks Japanese, said, "The Japanese really are too specific and it somehow hinders their initiative. You should have asked if he had any nine-hundred-and-seventy-yen CDs!"

You'll understand how refreshing it was when, while still in Yokohama, I put the same question to a different clerk: "Have you got any one-thousand-yen CDs?"

"No," he said. Then, after thinking carefully, he added, "But we have some for thirteen-hundred."

Japanese people with this kind of anticipation of a customer's needs, and the initiative to suggest an alternative, are most definitely in the minority.

Fitting the face to the hat

May 30, 1992

ON THE FIRST WARM DAY of this year, when I was feeling *genkier* than I normally do, I decided to discard my gray tweed jacket and flannel trousers in favor of a shirt and those Human Fit jeans I seem to recall telling you about. You know the jeans I mean — the ones that, had it not been for the "Human Fit" label, might have been construed as being a garment, tailored in Japan, for a giraffe.

I also donned my straw sun hat, and it is this I want to tell you about.

When I wore it, I looked like a cross between Crocodile Dundee and Roy Rogers, with a little bit of Pablo Picasso thrown in for good measure. It was a wonderful hat, and I felt especially good in it. My wife, who doubtless remembers how I'd bought it nine years ago for the equivalent of about ¥300 in a squalid market near Acapulco, Mexico, says it was dirty and old-looking. My daughter, meanwhile, recalls that the hat made me more handsome than I already am. For my part, I simply wore it to keep the sun off my head, which is what sun hats are generally for, isn't it?

I last donned that hat before leaving for a short trip to Totsuka, where I shopped for onions, shirt buttons, and a bottle of dish washing liquid. When I arrived at the station there, my attention was distracted by a scene that will remain indelible in my mind for as long as I remember Japan, which will doubtless be forever. Not too far from the drinks machine, opposite the pay telephones, were two elderly men. They had strewn a brown blanket on the cold, spit-spattered concrete floor and littered it with bento boxes and One-Cup Saké glasses.

From this, I presumed that they were homeless, and my heart reached out to them. That was until I remembered that in Japan, most people are such by choice. I'm not talking about those I met in Sanya, Tokyo's bottomless pit of despair, where several men were rendered unemployable when they fell drunk on the railway tracks one night and lost an arm or a leg to prove it. I'm referring to those who have created a little subculture on the edge of Japan's affluence, and seem to enjoy being a part of it. Otemachi Station has plenty of them, each of whom has laid claim to a little territory of his own in the long passageway that strikes up to Tokyo Station. There, every day, these men remove their shoes and rest on cardboard futon, having packed everything they own — mostly books, newspapers, and bottles — neatly into garbage bags in case they should suddenly be asked to move. They don't need hats because most of their lives are spent wandering that covered passageway.

As they do so, they are confident that no one — not even another homeless man — will ever venture into their space, for there are unwritten rules that govern common decency on the streets, especially in Japan where cultural traits are never forgotten or discarded. Only last week, for instance, I saw two homeless men sharing an electric razor they had probably plucked from the gomi. They had plugged it into a power source outside a flower shop and were taking turns shaving each other.

Anyway, as I swept through the ticket barrier at Totsuka Station, and past that row of pay telephones, a policeman approached the men. At this, one of them sprang to his feet and began to bow profusely, which meant he could not have been too drunk at all. The policeman, in turn, an immaculate, white-gloved figure in the bright mid-morning, made a brief but gentle speech that said, I believe, the men were not welcome where they were, and that they might drink their saké elsewhere.

One of them caught my eye as being special. He rose to a respectable height, bowed with grace, and was clad in a powder-blue summer suit that bore all the traces of having been donated by a considerably larger being. It was baggy and creased, but looked, nonetheless, to have been quite well-tailored. I'd say that this man was very definitely a cut above the kind of homeless souls who litter railway stations elsewhere — particularly those who shout obscenities at passers-by — because he possessed grace and nobility.

I did my shopping, then, returning to Totsuka Station two hours later, saw that despite the policeman's persuasive words, the men were still there. They were occupying my mind when I made a quick phone call home before rushing through the barrier and down the steps to catch my train. To my utter disappointment, I arrived home without my hat!

At first, I thought I had left it on the train. Then I recalled having placed it atop one of those telephones when I made that call. It was probably still there, I told myself repeatedly. Most people who lose things in Japan seem to get them back because, unlike all too many Westerners, who seem to find things before they are lost, the Japanese generally don't steal at all — unless they are politicians or real estate developers, in which case, they steal infinitely more than ordinary folks.

When I lived in Iogi, however, some ordinary person stole my bicycle. "No, no," says Hiroshi Sugiyama, who has lived in America. "He didn't steal it at all. He borrowed it and forgot to take it back. He probably even forgot where he'd taken it from and left it someplace else!"

Then someone "borrowed" my umbrella in a restaurant. "You should've locked it," says Hiroshi, with a shrug.

For all this, yet another friend, Noriyoshi Miyamoto, a professor at Bunkyo University, told me how he once lost ¥180,000 he had stuffed into a brown envelope. It was found near Yokohama Station by none other than a homeless man who — believe it or not — handed it to the police! "I tracked this fellow down," Professor Miyamoto remembers. "I thanked him, of course, from the bottom of my heart, then handed him a little reward. But he wouldn't take anything from me. He felt that to accept twenty-thousand yen just for being honest would be demeaning, and I understand this."

It is a heart-wrenching story indeed, and one that gave me some hope that it would not be too long before I saw my hat again. I was sure I'd get it back because, as I say, it was so grubby and misshapen — almost respectfully disgraceful, you might say — that no one else would have wanted it. I then discovered that the more I thought about it, the more I still liked it and I wanted it.

Was it to be? Back in Totsuka the other day, I sought directions to the station master's office to see if, by chance, the hat had been handed in. A ticket collector pointed the way — down the stairs into the basement. I went with mixed feelings. Halfway there, in fact, I asked myself how I would explain my dilemma. And who on earth tries to recover a battered hat that cost only ¥300? In Japan, you can't even buy two loaves of bread for that.

By now, I didn't care too much about the hat, at all, and it was just as well, for there, standing at his respectable height by the tobacco kiosk, was the man in the powder-blue suit. He carried a Sogo shopping bag this time and wore a new tie. But he was minus a shoe.

And on his head? No, it couldn't be! But it was!

He also wore my straw hat!

"I would have gone up to this guy," Hiroshi ventured when I told him the story, "and said, 'Excuse me for bothering you like this, but do you realize that what you have on your head doesn't belong to you because it happens to belong to me?' "

Then, after a pause, he added, "I'll get your hat back, if you really want me to. In the meantime, please buy your-self another hat — a more beautiful one. You can afford it. And anyway, you know that the guy that got your old one sure needed it, otherwise he would've handed it in at the lost property office."

Hiroshi was right, of course. In Totsuka, my Mexican straw hat had found a needy head — if not a deserving one — and I am feeling especially good about that.

Psychologist or fortune teller?

June 6, 1992

IF YOU FIND FOOD for thought in this week's column, you can thank my Roman Catholic priest friend who lives in Shin-Okubo, and who sent me the idea. He's a big block of a man, this priest, who wears running shoes and horn-rimmed glasses, and who wants to remain anonymous. He has been in Japan so long — about 40 years in all — that he has become very much a part of it, and has taken on some very Japanese traits.

One of these is that commendable thing called humility, the other the notion that if he were to be identified in any of my writings, he would stand out in the crowd, which might not be a good thing. The more I think about my priest friend, the more I think that with his special insights into human nature, and his marvelous sense of practicality, he should have written this column for me. It concerns a poor woman who recently aired her matrimonial woes in one of the English-language Japanese newspapers.

Allow me to point up some of the cultural disparities in a Japanese novelist's solution to this woman's plight, and mine.

> *Q: My 72-year-old husband is having an affair with a widow in her mid-60s. My husband has known this woman for a long time and became intimately involved with her after her husband died five years ago. He goes to see her*

227

almost every day, taking her food and other things from our house. Whenever I ask him about his relationship with her, he beats me until I'm black and blue.

I have asked my friends to talk to my husband and the woman, but they insist their relationship is only platonic. I have also asked our children to try to talk some sense into my husband, but nothing has changed.

The emotional pain is so strong that I have even thought about committing suicide. But I wouldn't want to embarrass my children by doing so.

I feel so depressed. Must I live out the rest of my life like this?

Mrs. R.
Kumamoto Pref.

The novelist who responded to this was a woman named Tei Fujiwara. I don't know what Miss Fujiwara's novels are like, but she is certainly no psychologist. In fact, I can't believe she would say some of the things she did — unless she was conforming to that little cultural quirk that drives a lot of us Westerners crazy. You know what I mean — that annoying habit a lot of Japanese people have of saying something, usually complimentary or upbeat, that they think the other person wants to hear at that particular moment.

In her reply, Miss Fujiwara sounds more like a fortune teller, hence my interjections, which I hope you will excuse.

Dear Mrs. R:
I am sure your husband will not listen to anything you have to say. He may have even forgotten your existence.

How can he do that, Miss Fujiwara? These two people still share the same house, don't they?

It is often said that love is blind. And when elderly people fall in love, they sometimes do unbelievable things because they can't control their emotions.

What kind of nonsense is this? Young people tend to be the ones who are more prone to stupidity in love. Actually, Miss Fujiwara, older people control their emotions far better than younger people because they have had more experience at it. Right? Anyway....

I know you are angry. But remember, this kind of romance can never last very long.

What do you mean by this, Miss Fujiwara? This relationship has been going on for five years, hasn't it? Isn't that long enough?

Your husband's affair with this widow will soon come to an end, and he will come back to you — burned out both physically and emotionally. I know this is a very trying time for you, but try to think that your husband has just contracted a fever. He will eventually be cured.

Give over, Miss Fujiwara! How do you know this five-year "fever," as you call it, will come to an end? And what makes you think that this woman's husband will crawl back to his wife "physically and emotionally burned out"? For all you know, he might be having one helluva good time, in which case he may well have no plans whatsoever to return. Has that crossed your mind?

If ever you meet this poor woman, or have occasion to write to her, you might like to pass on my advice with no holds barred — straight from the hip, so to speak — and with none of this "I-think-this-is-what-you-are-just-aching-to-hear" nonsense that does no one any good.

A: First, don't think about suicide. No other person is worth such a drastic step. And don't, whatever you do, hold your breath while waiting for your husband's affair to end. It's been going on for five years, remember. So resign yourself to the very strong possibility that he probably isn't coming back to you at all, at least not emotionally, particularly if he's enjoying himself.

The problem, of course, is that you aren't. You're fed up with the guy, and I don't blame you. He's let you down. He's cheated on you. By continuing to share the same house with him while he is having his affair, you are demeaning yourself and being made to look one huge fool in front of all intelligent people around you.

Now, there are some things you can do for yourself, and someone should point them out to you:

• The next time your husband beats you because you have confronted him about the other woman in his life, call the police. If they don't want to get involved in a domestic quarrel, which may well be the case, call me. Or better still, call my colleague Big Mike. He's pretty good at duffing people up.

On a second thought, maybe he and I should put the old guy in his place together!

• Don't confront your husband any more. You will be wasting your breath. Get yourself a bright young attorney who understands that some marriages just don't last and have the bastard legally ejected from your home so you can start living a proper life. That done, he won't give any more of your food to his mistress, or the other things you say he has been taking from the house to present to her. Not only that, it'll save you further beatings.

• Find someone else to share your life with. In this respect, you can ask your friends to help you. I could, too, except the only suitably-aged bachelor I know here in Tokyo is a burly, friendly, intelligent, fun-loving block of a man who wears horn-rimmed glasses and running shoes. He speaks Japanese — perfectly — but, unfortunately for you, happens to be a Roman Catholic priest.

Finally, remember that if you wait another five years for your husband to terminate his affair, too much time will have passed. He'll be 77, then, and you won't be any younger, either. So start living a proper life once again, before it is too late.

HOPE DOES NOT FADE for any of us, though — as is borne out by this little item listed in *Kentucky Marriages 1797–1865*, published by the Baltimore Genealogical Publishing Company:

On June 11, 1831, in Bath, Steuben County, N.Y., Moses Alexander married widow Frances Tompkins.

It was quite an event! He was 93, and she was 105.

The excitement, however, was awesome. The following morning, both Moses and Frances were found dead in their beds.

Music to my ears

June 6, 1992

IN TOKYO, WHERE, during the rush hour, a place to stand on a train — let alone sit — is hard to come by, you'd think that a railway man's lot would not be a particularly happy one. Well, for Iwao Sasaki it is, because he has made it so. He epitomizes Japanese pride in the job at hand. "You just think all the time of the customers," he says, his long, diamond-shaped face, topped by a generous carpet of gray hair, crinkling into a smile of contentment. "I mean, they're the most important people on Earth, aren't they?"

At an athletic 52, Sasaki is the station master at Shinagawa Station, a busy junction that sits on the southernmost tip of the Yamanote Line, and which services six other lines as well. Every day, 1,800 trains stop there and 420,000 people pour up its long steps, through its iron-girded corridors, and past its boutiques, kiosks, bars and noodle shops. Because half are leaving the station and the other half are arriving to catch their connections, most of the passengers are moving in opposite directions. But for all this, and it is certainly a commentary on the order of Japanese society, remarkably little untoward ever happens.

Why? Well, in January 1991, Iwao Sasaki and his staff of 300 met to discuss how they could make Shinagawa Station a better place to be — a sort of friendly drop-in center full of amenities but with relative tranquility.

233

The result? The other day, when I hurried through the station, as I do every morning, I heard bird noises. Intrigued, I walked around to see where the birds actually were. When I heard them chirping merrily in the men's washroom, I concluded that they must have been recorded. What bird in its right mind, after all, would want to live part of its little life in the men's washroom at Shinagawa Station?

Sasaki chuckles. Of course they were recorded. He likes bird songs — "they tranquilize passengers," he says — as he does music, and lots of it. His tastes run from *karaoke* and *enka* songs to popular ballads and Dixieland jazz, which, he concedes, is probably far too fast to play in a busy railway station. Selected pieces by the great masters aren't, though; the staff at that meeting also agreed to hire an outside firm to become the official Shinagawa Station Music Committee and provide what Sasaki calls "relaxing sounds that the public will enjoy whatever the time of day or night."

Good music, fellow railway men felt, might alleviate the pressures, and, of course, it does. On another recent morning, Mozart's *Clarinet Quintet* spilled from the speakers, and I have since listened to all manner of pieces by Bach, Handel, and Ravel.

The day I met Sasaki in his generous, wood-paneled office, with its clean gray carpet and great bank of potted plants, the CD system was pouring out a lavish, orchestral version of "You Light Up My Life." For the time I sat with the station master, drinking coffee and watching him puff preciously on a cigarette, he most certainly did just that.

"A few years ago," he says, "railway men seemed to

be a closed society. But now they are trying to change. They want to greet the people and make them happy." This is why, every month or so, the men set up a table at the top of the stairs that strike down to the Shinagawa Prince Hotel, specifically to hear customers' complaints.

There aren't that many, but what there are, Sasaki says, must be aired. So he puts on his gold-braided hat and white gloves, straightens his tie, makes sure there's still a shine on his black slip-on shoes, and goes to hear what his customers have to say, first-hand.

"One man said the staff wasn't polite enough," Sasaki remembers, his face suddenly solemn with disappointment. But all, it seems, said that they liked the bird songs and the music — "nothing too square," he adds, "just familiar, and nice and relaxing. And certainly no rock! That's too fast, and life around here is fast enough."

Unless someone falls down a flight of stairs, or is taken ill on a train, the biggest problem of all at Shinagawa Station occurs with clockwork regularity — at 1 a.m. each Saturday. That's when the last Yamanote Line train pulls in, and there is one drunk, invariably a disenchanted salaryman, in each of the 10 coaches.

A station master in, say, New York City or Chicago, would be worrying about someone slitting his throat at this time of night, but Sasaki's biggest worry is 10 harmless drunks who must be picked up and escorted — ticket or no ticket — through the barriers.

All who are on duty then, rise to the occasion with precision, compassion, and extraordinary punctilio — "Come this way, sir. Let me help you. You must be feeling very tired tonight, sir. May I take your arm and steady you a little?"

Don't be too amazed. All members of the Shinagawa Station staff have been trained to cope with such predicaments, including Iwao Sasaki himself.

He started his career cleaning engines when he was 19, but spent most of his time dreaming that he might one day have a station of his very own. It took him 31 of his 34 years with Japan Railways to achieve this — at Ofuna, south of Tokyo. But this was not until he had taken intensive company courses on how to develop good manners. Some railway men learn to be polite by being apprenticed to bellboys at large hotels, but Sasaki learned his diplomacy from JR executives.

Two years ago, after a stint in the company's planning division, he strolled into Shinagawa vowing to make changes there.

"And there's another problem," he says fretfully. "Pickpockets. Not many, but enough." And he shakes his head.

His biggest worry recently, however, was when a white plastic bag blew onto the overhead power line along the tracks near Osaki Station, shutting down the entire Yamanote Line for the best part of 40 minutes — during rush hour. "That," Sasaki says, "was terrible. We all felt we'd let the public down."

He wonders about this, too, when, during peak hours, a lot of those 420,000 passengers who board or leave those 1,800 trains at Shinagawa each day, become frustrated when they can't find a place to stand, and accuse other passengers of needlessly shoving them around.

When a fist fight ensues, Station Master Sasaki assigns an assistant to call the police, then puts on his hat and gloves once more and sees what he can do to defuse the tension himself.

He does this almost every day, mostly in the mornings. Fights at the height of the evening rush hour, however, are invariably the responsibility of someone else. By then, usually at around 5:30 p.m., and as the traffic swells, Iwao Sasaki has hung up his gold-braided hat, shed his bright blue uniform, and changed into a gray suit. Now, he has joined the madding crowds himself, and is scurrying up or down grimy station steps to board either the Yokosuka Line or the Tokaido Line. He is on his way home to Kawasaki, not far from where his career started out.

"I never get a seat," he says with quiet resolve. "I stand up, hang on, and read my newspaper."

No one would suspect that this amiable father of two, who likes fishing, bicycling, enka, and plain good manners — and who believes that bird songs should spill out in the men's washroom — presides over the Tokyo area's ninth largest railway station. But he does, with pleasure. "We've got to make this place even better," he says.

A labor of love

June 13, 1992

"Excuse me," said the young woman I met at a dinner party a few weeks ago, "may I ask you a question?" I said she could. I have spent more than two-thirds of my life answering questions. Why not another one now?

"Well," she said, "I've been wondering. How do you write a column?"

"With difficulty, madam," I said with reckless abandon. "And sometimes with *great* difficulty."

"Oh," the woman said, surprised. "I thought it would be so easy for you!"

On my way home, I decided that my reply had been a little flippant, and that the question wasn't such a bad one after all. I had imparted the general idea, I think, that when I am at dinner parties, I do not like to talk about my work. Yet I enjoy it. In fact, I can't see myself doing anything else with my life right now. One of the other things I have learned in 35 years of writing, though, is that writing is best ministered and not spoken about. In any case, there are so many things about it that just cannot be easily explained in a few words.

"I've got a great story!" I would announce at my first newspaper, *The Sheerness Times Guardian*, back in England in the late 1950s.

"Don't tell me," the news editor invariably muttered, tersely. "Write the bloody thing!"

So I did. I slaved for hours, it seemed, putting

sentences into paragraphs, then shuffling the paragraphs into some kind of order. Then I decided they were all in the wrong order, and started the entire process all over again. Today, I am happy to tell you, I don't have that worry. The shape, or the architecture, of writing — the most important element of it, in fact — as well as the words, and the nuance and tone these can be made to create, come much more naturally to me. So do the thoughts and the use of anecdotes that are needed to animate writing, and give it character.

What *doesn't* come easily to me are ideas, and this is especially true in Japan, where those who choose to write columns or feature articles for English-language newspapers and magazines find themselves with two separate reading audiences that have a difference in needs as wide as the Grand Canyon.

That difference must be met, head-on, and doing it can be a tricky business. There is no point, for instance, telling anyone what they already know about Japan. There is, however, every good reason to try to explain a facet of this intriguing country to foreigners while telling the Japanese what is right and wrong with it at the same time.

The other day, a young American telephoned to say how much he was enjoying my recent book, and made the simple observation, "You are better when you are upbeat." (Actually, he also called to share a visa problem with me, and I like to think that I gave him "upbeat" advice on the matter.) Other readers who have also commented on my work have said I am better when I write humorously, and I probably am.

Enter another problem, and a big one: Humor,

which is extremely difficult to write in the first place, does not always cross ethnic borders. What might make Westerners laugh may not necessarily amuse the Japanese, and usually doesn't. To compensate for this, then, a humorous column needs to have other levels, other dimensions; while some readers will, indeed, chuckle at it, others will understand the sociological commentary behind it, or grasp some of its ironies.

Ah, irony! Without this, and anecdotes and strong, active writing, a column can be as flat as a desert. And here's another point I must constantly remember: Readers don't want their columnists to be news reporters. Nor do they want to be served one-dimensional topics that have nothing to commend them other than their being off-beat, unusual, or just plain silly. Good columns must have more to them than this.

Above all, readers expect an opinion in a column, a point of view — something they can latch onto and savor. In the West, where columnists are part of a strong tradition, they have been known to carve entire careers out of being disliked for what they say, while others have thrived on being trusted and admired. Rarely can a columnist afford to sit somewhere in between. No one likes writers who do not commit themselves, who sit on the fence, so to speak, and who avoid controversy at all cost. Readers swoop upon the chance to either agree or disagree with a columnist, just as — subconsciously — they want to love him or hate him.

It is ironic that columnists who dare to speak the truth for the betterment of their fellow men and women can be reviled for doing just that.

"So, how do you choose your topics?" the woman persisted.

"With difficulty, madam," I said again.

First, instinct comes into play, and by the time a writer has entered his middle years, and with solid experience behind him, this is usually fairly astute. A former colleague editor at *Time* magazine used to say, "If something makes you laugh or cry, write it immediately. Just make sure that it makes others laugh or cry, too, that's all!" I have never forgotten this. Nor will I forget the words of another editor, with whom I worked for nearly 10 years at *Reader's Digest.* "Topics for all good writing," he said, "need to contain elements of lasting importance in the first place, yet be entertaining in the second. They must also be of broad and enduring interest."

The most important thing I have learned, on my own, no less, is that good writing always seems to look so deceptively simple — like a Grandma Moses painting or a little Mozart piano sonata.

The moment an idea for a column has descended on me, nearly always in its rawest form, I spend many hours thinking about it. I spin it around many times in my head, viewing it from all angles, and wondering how it can best be explained and what characters will help bring it to life for readers to enjoy. That accomplished, my raw idea may indeed become a *wonderful* idea! In this case, I will be absolutely obsessed with it until it is written.

With what I want to say — and how I want to say it — clear in my mind, the words will inevitably flow a little easier when I seat myself before my IBM-compatible portable computer. For all this, though, each of my columns takes six hours to write, and sometimes more. Since most are composed at home after a daily grind of editing other people's work, they really are — like a lot of other things that go on at *The Weekly* — truly a labor of love.

As such, I let my columns say exactly what I feel. Writers who aspire to perform their craft impeccably must never allow the mindless, the useless, the jealous, or the unimaginative to taint their work, no matter how much they may try to do so. I don't. I pour out my feelings obliviously, imperviously, totally intent on satisfying readers.

To find my topics, I search the corners of everything I can set my eyes upon, from newsletters and pamphlets to advertisements and books, hoping that something will spark my imagination. Add to this process what I hear, see, know, feel, and think, and you'll have some idea of just how most of my ideas are born, and how they inevitably take on a personal slant. What you have almost finished reading, which took part of last Saturday and almost all of Sunday, in fact, stemmed entirely from one curious woman's not-too-curious question — "How do you write a column?"

Now, I hope, she will know. What she may not be aware of, however, is that the politics of being a columnist is not the most pleasant side of the business at all. When readers' letters come in, though, the work of a man like me —who is condemned to his room for so long, with nothing but his language — becomes eminently worthwhile.

Don't rock the boat!

June 20, 1992

LET'S TAKE OFF OUR HATS to a Japanese journalist who
has the courage to agree that there is something
distinctly rotten about his country's print journalism,
and that it should be better. "Japanese newspapers,"
writes Takeshi Maezawa, "bind themselves with taboos
and rarely engage in serious investigative reporting.
Most major scandals over the past 15 years, with the
exception of the Recruit bribes-for-political-favors
scandal, were first disclosed by media other than newspapers, or by the foreign press." Even when Japanese
newspapers were first with an important story, Maezawa
says, they rarely ran them before the results of inves-
tigations were leaked.

On top of all this, Japanese reporters customarily
cultivate tight, exclusive relationships with politicians
and bureaucrats — while editorial committee members
at major Japanese newspapers sit on government
advisory councils. This, Maezawa contends, means that
if ever editors want to criticize the government, they
can't.

Now, I've never met a Japanese journalist who has
felt inclined to call the government to task. Why,
exactly? And why don't those Japanese people already
in journalism learn more about it and develop journalistic
judgment?

The reasons are numerous. First, the men who run

243

Japan's newspapers and magazines know very little about modern-day journalism and what it should do. Oh, they know their publications must make money, of course. But they are not quite sure what should go in them, and in what form. Consequently, they never speak in terms of "sharp, crisp news stories" or "powerful, human features." Nor do they prescribe "stinging editorials." On the contrary, they are more apt to tell their staffers to make articles and headings as dull as they possibly can so as not to upset the establishment. "Keep it wooden," they so often say. "Don't rock the boat!"

To young people who are fresh to the business, and who know no better, these men are dreadful role models. In the West, reporters learn very early how absolutely not to make writing wooden. And if they persist in making it so, they lose their jobs. The purpose of print journalism, after all, is to reveal the real world accurately and faithfully with solid, pertinent facts delivered in a lively writing style that will attract and inform a lot of readers. Only in Japan, it seems, where newspapers are edited by salarymen and not by properly trained editors, is "wooden" writing perfectly honorable.

That's not all. Over the years, Japanese publishers, editors, and reporters, have all allowed government and big business to dictate to them. They have let them interfere with the way a story is to be told, or if it is to be told at all. About a year ago, the magazine Themis folded after its owner had bowed to government pressure to kill a story that was supposedly critical of the Tax Agency. No proper publisher who considered his readers would have given in so easily. He would have fought for what is right and published the story anyway. So, when the government ordered him to close down, maybe he got what he deserved. In a democracy, which journalism must help refine and protect, publishers cannot afford to be told what to put in their magazines.

This business of letting outside forces control information explains why the source of far too much of what is printed in Japan's newspapers is, as you will have noticed, a government or industrial report. In the West, reporters are taught to be wary of these because they might just be propaganda, which they so often are. In Japan, though, attitudes to authority dictate that whatever officials say, should be printed almost without question.

This has been going on for so long, that both government and industry have effectively tamed Japanese reporters. Thus press conferences are rarely what they are supposed to be — confrontational. Reporters simply write exactly what they are told to, carefully avoiding any kind of controversy. An American ecologist told me how she attended a press conference at which angry Japanese environmentalists were to have confronted Japan's environment minister. "But when the time came for them to do it," she recalls, "everyone just sat there nodding their heads. They didn't ask a single question. Nor did the newspaper reporters, come to that."

Never mind big business and governments controlling information. Takeshi Maezawa remembers news coverage being censored by Japanese traditions and superstitions! Last October, a *Yomiuri Shimbun* reporter was denied access to a celebration marking the completion of a highway tunnel in Yamagata because the workers honestly believed the presence of a woman would "anger the goddess of the mountain" and cause a critical accident. Despite repeated requests to cover the ceremonial speeches and take photographs of the guests, the woman was led away.

Censorship is also encouraged by the legal system, it seems. When another *Yomiuri* reporter entered the Kanazawa District Court to cover a class-action suit against a nuclear power station, she found that the chief judge had posted an injunction prohibiting news gathering in the court house. Exercising her news sense, the woman tried to photograph this notice. As she did so, about 10 courtroom officials obeyed the judge's orders and stood menacingly in her way.

Both this, and the case of the mountain "goddess" were eventually resolved. The Highway Public Corporation convinced the construction companies that built the tunnel that "goddesses" actually like women reporters, and the Kanazawa court judge apologized for his "inappropriate" action. But the damage had been done. Readers were deprived of important facts that were undeniably the public's right to know.

Questions still remain, however, about whether this kind of thing will ever happen again and, if it does, to what lengths Japan's journalists are prepared to go to fight it. None, I suspect. But if they want to upgrade their profession to conform to Western standards, and thereby help to "internationalize" their country as they go, they must cast off some of their cultural niceties and start telling governments and big business that, for the sake of democracy, they must no longer interfere.

Perhaps the biggest reason why Japanese journalism is ineffectual is this: Proper journalism calls for an objectively critical view of the world, so, to gather those pertinent facts, a certain amount of confrontation is often required. Neither of these qualities, of course, comes naturally to the Japanese. The moment they start school, they are taught to obey, not to contest; to follow, not to lead; to be grateful for what they have, even though this may not be very much, and not to fight for more; to honor authority, no matter how questionable it may be, and not to cause its downfall. Children grow up impervious to their country's faults, believing that if they protect their culture and preserve a non-critical environment, they will automatically be led forth to prosperity.

Unfortunately, such teachings do not spawn journalists, and never did. The kind of journalism that inspires or motivates, or forces governments to make a system more equitable, requires a talent for investigation. And all investigation is predicated on the simple assumption that people — particularly politicians — are not always truthful.

Proper journalism, then, is no place for the superstitious or the wide-eyed. People who think that racism, sexism, or chauvinism are fine, or that single-parent women should continue to be victimized, or that key money is not an unwarranted gift to a greedy landlord, or that gray-haired old men with no apparent ability — like some of the editors Takeshi Maezawa and I both know — should be free to manipulate men and women who are more talented than themselves, or that nothing need ever be done to change these things, then journalism is not for them.

They would best serve their country by finding something else to do.

Trouble at the sento

June 20, 1992

IN MOST CIVILIZED countries, what I am about to tell you would not only be considered repugnant by all decent people, but be actionable in the highest court in the land — for being racism at its very worst. If you are appalled by it, so you should be.

As more foreigners arrive in Japan to teach English, or to work as entertainers, laborers, or in any other job the Japanese would prefer not to do themselves, the clientele at public baths and hot springs have become somewhat cosmopolitan. But the traditional Japanese users of these quiet, steamy places have grown increasingly unhappy about having to share the same water with people who are not like themselves.

These four-tatami xenophobes, as I call them, have made their views known not only to their friends, who have stopped bathing there, but to the bath owners themselves, who are bowing to the pressure — and the prejudice.

Last month, a public bath in Kofu, Yamanashi Prefecture, posted a sign that announced: "No foreigners allowed." So neither the British Ambassador, nor the American Ambassador, nor the Duke of Edinburgh, nor the President of the United States, nor Pope John, nor myself, could use the place had we wanted to. None of us looks Japanese, or behaves in a Japanese way, and this means that each of us is a "Them," and certainly

249

not an "Us." And in all too many Japanese eyes, the "Thems" of this crazy mixed-up world are downright dirty folks.

In most civilized countries, where minorities are inevitably protected by laws, the owner of this bath, or *sento*, would be prosecuted so quickly his feet would not touch the ground. But that has not been the case here. In fairness, I must point out that the Kofu Health Center — and not its legal department, by the way — did advise the bath's owners (somewhat gently, for this is the Japanese way), to remove the sign, and this they did. But the discrimination continued. Non-Japanese bathers were told they were not welcome.

This is not an isolated case. In December, a hotel in Komoro, Nagana Prefecture, posted a sign announcing that the hot springs there could not be used by those foreigners residing in Japan illegally. How the staff establishes whether residents are "legal" or not, without checking their passports, is a mystery to me. The sign also said that "people who look like gangsters" were prohibited from bathing there, and this is a bigger mystery. Presumably the management has a clear idea of how gangsters are supposed to look, so woe betide anyone who happens to have a pudgy nose and cauliflower ears, especially if he happens to be a Shinto priest or an actuary.

"You a gangster, buddy?"

"Naaah, not today. And never in an *onsen*."

Anyway, this week, the Komoro Health Center was insisting that all people should be allowed to use the hotel's hot springs — all foreigners, regardless of the status of their visas, and all Al Capones or Bugsy Siegels, which is the good news. The bad news is that the people most angered by the sign are not the district's real-life gangsters, but the real-life wives — most of them Koreans and Filipinos — of local Japanese. They are not so good at asserting themselves as hoods.

Imagine how they felt when, as they dipped their toes in the water — even after having showered and done all the other things females are supposed to do before stepping into a public bath — a group of four-tatami-minded Japanese women climbed out, vowing never to return. That's when the hotel's management decided to take what it called "countermeasures."

"We posted the sign because we wanted our facilities to be widely used by local residents," an official explained. "We also wanted to provide a place for bathing in which Japanese customs could be observed. We had no intention of banning all foreigners."

Maybe not, but the sign is still there — and it grows more offensive by the day.

In defense of these bath proprietors, it could be said that they are so under-evolved that they know no better. No one has yet bothered to explain to them what racism is, so they may not be totally responsible for perpetuating it. Unfortunately, however, racism is easily taught, and the philosophy of running places that are solely for "Us" and not for "Them" — because the "Thems" look different — has been so well learned, that it has spread, as you know, into other corners of Japanese society. There is nothing subtle about it, yet I have not heard of any official body doing anything about stopping it once and for all.

Affixed to the doors of several real estate offices in

some of the larger cities in Chiba Prefecture, for instance, are signs that say: "We don't negotiate leases for foreigners." One actually says, "We don't deal with foreigners at all, so they shouldn't bother coming in."

"When I first saw it," says colleague columnist Naoko Nishiwaki, "I wanted to tell the manager to take it down because, as a Japanese, I was offended by it. There are many foreigners among my friends, and I would rent my house to any of them, at any time. I decided to do nothing about the sign, though. If people want to tell the world they're racists, that's their problem."

Back in Kofu, a woman named Masako Tanaka feels this way, too. She runs a hot-spring bath her father, 72-year-old Tsutomu Tanaka, first opened back in 1928. Everything was fine until about a year ago, when foreigners started turning up, and Masako, 42, began to hear the first discontent from disgruntled customers — "We don't want to come to your bath anymore."

One woman told her, "We believe it's better not to go into the same water as those other people have been in. No matter how much they deny having AIDS, you'll never know the truth. And you don't know what other diseases they might be carrying." Another woman, also with a four-tatami mentality, asked Masako, "Who will you choose, us or them?"

Masako, bless her, took nearly everyone in the quiet, working-class neighborhood by complete surprise when she decided to support the "Thems." Some foreigners, she admitted, had failed to rinse their bodies before stepping into the bath, while others had been caught bathing in their underwear! But usually, she said, these matters were resolved when the offenders were given a few quiet instructions on the etiquette of Japanese bathing. Meanwhile, she visited the Kofu Health Center and Japan's Public Bath Association and collected a slew of leaflets that explained, among other things, that no one has yet caught AIDS from washing themselves with other people, nor will they.

Even after pinning these leaflets on her notice board, her clientele continued to dwindle. Masako and her father agreed that if they lost any more customers they might have to close their bath down. They still decided, however — at a family meeting attended by brothers and sisters and uncles and aunts, all of whom sat bolt upright on the floor sipping green tea — that banning foreign bathers would be "morally wrong, and a very cruel thing to do."

"A public bath," Masako declared, "is for people — all people — who don't have a proper bath in their homes."

This is what she wrote in a letter she mailed to her regular clients. "The problem," she added, "is best solved by teaching foreigners about our culture and customs. Isn't that what kindness is all about?"

It is, of course. So the next time you are in a sento or an onsen, think of Masako Tanaka, please. We need a few more folks like her, and a few less pushy people with four-tatami minds who, if they persist in acting the way they do, will make Bugsy Siegel and Al Capone appear more like cherubs than the hoods they really were.

Whiskey, karaoke – and me
Unpublished

WELL, I DON'T REMEMBER too much about getting home on Saturday night, or very much about what was said just before I departed, come to that. This is because when my wife and I met Gikon Tamaki for supper, he ordered an inexhaustible supply of beer, then decided we should both try some hot saké. But that wasn't the end of it. Not by any means.

We were in Ofuna, which lies to the south of Yokohama, in one of those little restaurants where there is barely room to swing a small monkey. We could have sat on the tatami around a coffee table, but because I have the terrible fear that I might one day sit on a floor and never be able to get up, we agreed to eat at the counter — Irene and I, and Gikon and his friend Saint Masa, who is so named because he doesn't smoke or drink, and never tells a lie. Well, not big ones, anyway.

Saint Masa, I seem to recall, was talking about one of his school chums, former Prime Minister Yasuhiro Nakasone, and Gikon was telling me that while playing for the Totsuka old timers' baseball team two Sundays ago, he pitched three innings without giving up a hit. Apparently, Gikon also stole third base from first, and one of his teammates hit an infield home run. That's because the ball became lodged in a wire fence and two of the outfielders on the opposing team had awful problems getting it out.

Decide for yourself what kind of game this was. Who steals two bases in one attempt? Who can't retrieve a ball from a fence?

Anyway, the highlight of our evening in Ofuna was when the cook, a man named Kazu who did so much high-speed chopping behind the counter I thought he'd go home minus some of his fingers, made a quick telephone call and then addressed our group in impeccable English.

"When you have all finished here," he announced, "Tamaki-san will take you to a bar where you will find a bottle of whiskey and a shrimp pizza waiting — a present from me. I will be there later to sing a song."

I thought this was kind, but Gikon seemed strangely unmoved by it. "Kazu-san says we can drink his whiskey," he said with a shrug. So off we went.

The bar was empty when he arrived there, except for two very well-scrubbed women who seated us and produced the pizza. There, too, was Kazu's whiskey — the bottle he'd bought for whenever he went in there himself, which was every night after taking down the *noren* outside his restaurant. At least, I think that's the way it works. The bottle, now on the big, curved, oak counter, lives on a shelf behind the bar with about 50 others, and bears a brass name tag I couldn't read.

I wasn't into reading anyway. Saint Masa, who'd finally succumbed to a little saké and said he didn't much like Nakasone, decided to excuse himself when one of the women turned on the *karaoke* machine — and when Gikon rose to sing a song. At that point, I wanted to leave, too. But then, to my dismay, Irene reminded Gikon that I'd once been an opera tenor, whereupon

the owner of the bar, a willowy woman with little gold-
framed glasses and an abundance of hair heaped onto
the top of her head, presented me with a list of songs
— the only English songs in the system.

There they were — all the old standbys — and, at
first, I felt comfortable about singing only one of them:
"I Left My Stupid Heart in God-forsaken San Francisco." Despite being on my third whiskey, because
Gikon kept signaling to have my glass topped up, I gave
what I thought was a fairly honorable rendition of it. At
the end, I hit a ringing high-C, and, before I knew it,
a lot of people had poured in from the steamy night to
see what all the fuss was about.

Not one of them spoke any English, so I didn't know
what they really thought. What I *did* know was that the
list of English karaoke songs had come back to me for
a second perusal. I also knew I was getting drunker than
I wanted to be because one of those songs was "Diana,"
and I allowed myself to be persuaded to bestow a lusty,
operatic treatment upon this, too, even though it was
in a low key, and tenors are much happier with higher
ones.

I never thought I'd sing "Diana." Not in Ofuna. The
last time I appeared in public, in a concert organized
by a Totsuka voice teacher, I sang three Italian art
songs, and was accompanied by a woman at a Steinway.
I'd planned on that occasion to perform a big aria from
Donizetti's opera *Lucia di Lammermoor* but decided against
it, remembering the words of an old bass-baritone I'd
met some years ago — "Always sing something you feel
comfortable with and can do well. People inevitably
remember when you sing badly."

Contrary to this advice, I poured out "Diana" as I thought dear Diana would have liked it, then had two more whiskeys and watched even more people traipse into the bar, until most of them could find nowhere to sit. Gikon seized upon the moment to sing another song, and this is doubtless why the list came back to me.

Rock numbers aren't my style either, so I left them to a plump young man who had been sleeping two seats away from me. He awoke, did a fairly commendable job on two of them, then went back to sleep. Nor am I any good at "Jealousy," which is why I let a shriveled, gray-haired woman by the door do that one. And she wasn't bad, either. Her voice was a bit shrill and wobbly for my taste, but it didn't seem to matter. People in Ofuna like listening to human birds.

Finally, at the bottom of the hand-written list, I came upon "Danny Boy," an old karaoke stalwart, and a song I hated as much as "Diana," until I once sang it somewhere in Hakone. In that Ofuna bar, however, I gave this old number such a royal and robust treatment that I had to sing it again — not so much to get it right, but because the folks wanted to sing it with me. Someone then asked me what else I could sing. So I had to perform "I Left My Drunken Heart in Stupid San Francisco" again, and suddenly, after the applause had died down, everyone in that dark, plush little bar, who were almost as well-oiled as I was, spoke the best English they'd ever spoken in their lives.

The woman who'd sung like a bird elbowed her way through the people and told she had heard Domingo and Pavarotti bring dow n packed houses in London.

"Can you sing 'O Sole Mio' like *they* can?" she kept

asking. "Or 'Come Back to Sorrento'?" And the man who had been sleeping said he didn't much like rock music anyway, and harbored a secret passion for Russian love songs.

That's when I decided I'd had quite enough for one night. I didn't come to Ofuna to sing about Danny, Diana, and San Francisco, I recall telling myself as I stumbled onto the last train.

On Sunday, when I awoke with an atrocious hangover, I decided I actually hated Danny, Diana, and San Francisco as much as I disliked drinking. And if I were ever to sing in a karaoke bar again, I would have to know some Japanese songs, so I could be just like Gikon Tamaki. At least I should be able to perform "My Way" like Kazu the kindly cook.